Institut für Buchkunst Leipzig | Scheidegger & Spiess

Published by Scheidegger & Spiess in cooperation with the Institut für Buchkunst Leipzig,
Prof. Ludovic Balland, Julia Blume

THE PRESIDENT OF THE UNITED STATES ON SCREEN

in Motion Pictures, Series, and on TV

A Compendium by Lea N. Michel

TABLE OF CONTENTS

p. 7 Alternative Table of Contents I–VI
[A Typology of Presidents]

p. 47 Categories A–W
[Presidents in Illustrations]

p. 435 United Presidents of America
[Essay by Teresa Rudolf]

p. 443 Index Presidents 1–164
[Presidents, Movies/Series, Years, Actors, and Illustration Index]

Alternative Table of Contents I–VI
[A Typology of Presidents]

The Father and Husband
[type one]

[scene] I.I

p. 230 in bed with his wife

p. 232 in the bathroom

p. 334 shaving

p. 382 washing his face

p. 179 in a bathrobe

p. 345 singing

p. 132 getting dressed

[scene] I.II

p. 236 in the kitchen

p. 111 drinking coffee

p. 317 reading the newspaper

p. 164 having breakfast
p. 411 with his family
p. 366 talking to his daughter
p. 132 getting a promise from
his daughter
p. 177 hugging his daughter

[scene] I.III

p. 208 in a meeting at the
Oval Office
p. 289 on the telephone
p. 425 working
p. 71 behind the desk in
the Oval Office
p. 342 signing files
p. 164 hanging a picture in
the Oval Office
p. 262 looking at memories

[scene] I.IV

p. 302 out for a hike
p. 358 talking to a boy
p. 396 with a dog

p. 125 fishing
p. 306 playing baseball
p. 119 eating
p. 307 playing golf

[scene] I.V

p. 92 boarding Air Force One
p. 383 watching TV
p. 368 talking to the press
p. 142 getting out of
Air Force One, waving

[scene] I.VI

p. 201 in a kindergarten
p. 310 playing Scrabble
p. 392 with a child
p. 156 giving an interview
with his wife

[scene] I.VII

p. 60 at a banquet
p. 413 with his wife
p. 158 greeting a crowd

p. 330 shaking hands
p. 190 in a conversation
p. 386 waving

[scene] I.VIII

p. 289 on the telephone
p. 335 shocked
p. 173 his wife holding his face
p. 105 crying

[scene] I.IX

p. 241 in the Oval Office
talking to his staff
p. 349 sitting on the desk in
the Oval Office
p. 51 addressing the
nation on TV
p. 99 broadcast on TV

[scene] I.X

p. 146 giving a press conference
p. 174 hugging his family
p. 352 smiling

[scene] I.XI

p. 95 bowling

p. 120 eating cake

p. 408 with his daughter

The Villain
[type two]

[scene] II.I

p. 67 at the inauguration
p. 158 greeting a crowd
p. 150 giving a speech
p. 370 targeted by a gun
p. 126 fleeing
p. 135 getting into a car

[scene] II.II

p. 202 in a meeting
p. 71 behind the desk in the Oval Office
p. 407 with feet on the table

p. 355 smoking
p. 95 briefing staff

[scene] II.III

p. 410 with his double
p. 284 on board a ship
p. 229 in bed with his mistress
p. 250 kissing
p. 135 getting his nose licked
p. 179 in a bathrobe

[scene] II.IV

p. 253 kissing his mistress
p. 226 in bed
p. 48 abusing a woman
p. 250 killing
p. 401 with a knife
p. 394 with a dead body

[scene] II.V

p. 247 injured
p. 423 with the Secret Service
p. 81 being briefed

p. 105 concerned
p. 113 drinking alcohol
p. 179 in a bathrobe

[scene] II.VI
p. 131 gambling
p. 309 playing pool
p. 412 with his mistress

[scene] II.VII
p. 163 greeting the military
p. 190 in a conversation
p. 360 talking to a high-ranking officer
p. 54 angry
p. 220 in a video conference
p. 427 working late

[scene] II.VIII
p. 230 in bed with his wife

[scene] II.IX
p. 320 riding a motorbike

p. 389 wearing sunglasses
p. 256 listening to music
p. 431 working out
p. 255 lifting weights

[scene] II.X
p. 368 talking to the press
p. 296 on TV
p. 157 giving someone the finger

[scene] II.XI
p. 393 with a crashed helicopter
p. 404 with a signal flare
p. 57 as a hostage
p. 419 with the nuclear code
p. 257 locked up
p. 374 threatened with a weapon

[scene] II.XII
p. 123 fighting
p. 391 with a bust of Lincoln

[scene] II.XIII

p. 171 **hiding**
p. 64 **at a graveyard**
p. 399 **with a gun**
p. 338 **shooting**

[scene] II.XIV

p. 108 **dead**

The Alien
[type three]

[scene] III.I

p. 51 addressing the nation on TV

p. 59 as an alien

p. 281 on board Air Force One

p. 140 getting out of Air Force One

p. 284 on the cell phone

[scene] III.II

p. 278 on a stage

p. 103 campaigning

p. 404 with a superhero

p. 304 photographed by the press
p. 150 giving a speech

[scene] III.III
p. 374 threatened with a weapon
p. 327 screaming

[scene] III.IV
p. 125 fighting with a lightsaber
p. 402 with an alien

[scene] III.V
p. 126 fleeing
p. 198 in a helicopter
p. 416 with the nuclear briefcase

[scene] III.VI
p. 202 in a meeting
p. 421 with the officer who is
carrying the nuclear briefcase
p. 181 in a bunker
p. 81 being briefed
p. 406 with confidential files

[scene] III.VII

p. 229 in bed with her husband

p. 362 talking to her husband

[scene] III.VIII

p. 241 in the Oval Office talking to her staff

p. 247 incredulous

p. 312 reading files

p. 160 greeting foreign politicians

p. 220 in a video conference

p. 429 working on a computer

p. 113 drinking alcohol

[scene] III.IX

p. 261 looking at a spaceship

p. 202 in a lab

[scene] III.X

p. 361 talking to an inmate

p. 56 as a hologram

p. 276 on a phone screen

[scene] III.XI

p. 69 awarding an officer
p. 321 saluting
p. 415 with robot arms
p. 150 giving a speech
p. 296 on TV

[scene] III.XII

p. 262 looking at memories
p. 71 behind the desk in
the Oval Office
p. 366 talking to her daughter
p. 177 hugging her daughter
p. 174 hugging her son
p. 254 laughing

The Clown
[type four]

[scene] IV.I

p. 143 getting out of the car

p. 161 greeting guests at a banquet

p. 60 at a banquet

p. 382 washing dentures in the glass of another politician

[scene] IV.II

p. 110 dressed as a woman

p. 113 drinking alcohol

p. 106 dancing

p. 56 as a DJ

p. 380 vomiting

[scene] IV.III

p. 277 on a sign
p. 390 with a bridal bouquet

[scene] IV.IV

p. 349 sitting on the desk in the Oval Office
p. 219 in a tracksuit
p. 119 eating
p. 358 taking his shoes off
p. 334 sharpening a pencil in his ear
p. 214 in a meeting with the military
p. 275 offering candies

[scene] IV.V

p. 226 in bed
p. 275 naked
p. 390 with a balloon animal
p. 258 looking at a globe
p. 81 being briefed
p. 281 on a tin can telephone

[scene] IV.VI

p. 198 in a floating fridge
p. 357 swimming
p. 110 diving

[scene] IV.VII

p. 351 sleeping
p. 294 on the telephone in bed
p. 427 working in bed
p. 272 making smoke rings
p. 312 reading files

[scene] IV.VIII

p. 190 in a conversation
p. 410 with his double
p. 116 drinking milk
p. 116 drinking through a straw

[scene] IV.IX

p. 281 on board Air Force One
p. 431 working out
p. 121 eating chicken wings
with another politician

[scene] IV.X

p. 146 giving a press conference
p. 296 on TV
p. 173 holding up a dog's ears
p. 406 with dentures
p. 346 sitting behind the desk
addressing the nation
p. 433 wrapped in a blanket

[scene] IV.XI

p. 76 behind his desk in
the Oval Office,
talking to the staff
p. 407 with feet on the table
p. 383 watching TV
p. 119 eating

[scene] IV.XII

p. 272 meeting another
politician
p. 218 in a school class
p. 391 with a bust of Lincoln
p. 307 playing basketball

[scene] IV.XIII

p. 156 giving a speech at
the United Nations

p. 275 naked

p. 356 speaking to a crowd
with a megaphone

p. 157 giving someone the finger

p. 321 riding a pig

The Hero [type five]

[scene] V.I

p. 88 bloodied
p. 86 being sworn in
p. 233 in the crashed
Air Force One
p. 415 with the military

[scene] V.II

p. 138 getting out of a helicopter
p. 423 with the Secret Service
p. 386 waving
p. 304 photographed by
the press

[scene] V.III

p. 346 sitting behind the desk

p. 51 addressing the nation

[scene] V.IV

p. 212 in a meeting room

[scene] V.V

p. 69 at the United Nations

p. 272 meeting another politician

[scene] V.VI

p. 143 getting out of the car

p. 65 at a state reception

p. 160 greeting foreign politicians

p. 330 shaking hands

p. 146 giving a press conference

[scene] V.VII

p. 183 in a car

p. 362 talking to his son

p. 119 eating

[scene] V.VIII

p. 71 behind the desk in the Oval Office

p. 81 being briefed

[scene] V.IX

p. 312 reading files

p. 76 behind his desk in the Oval Office, talking to the staff

p. 342 signing files

p. 289 on the telephone

[scene] V.X

p. 349 sitting on the desk in the Oval Office

p. 105 concerned

p. 113 drinking alcohol

p. 260 looking at a screen

p. 295 on the telephone, looking at files

p. 311 reading a note

p. 433 writing

[scene] V.XI

p. 60 at a banquet
p. 150 giving a speech
p. 370 targeted by a gun
p. 377 under fire
p. 171 hiding
p. 216 in a restaurant kitchen
p. 126 fleeing
p. 90 boarding a helicopter

[scene] V.XII

p. 181 in a bunker
p. 244 in the Situation Room
p. 214 in a meeting with the military
p. 196 in a crisis situation
p. 263 looking at military strategies
p. 223 in a video conference with a terrorist

[scene] V.XIII

p. 188 in a control center

p. 270 looking shocked at a screen
p. 288 on the red telephone

[scene] V.XIV
p. 239 in the office on board
Air Force One
p. 57 as a hostage
p. 257 locked up
p. 374 threatened with a weapon

[scene] V.XV
p. 416 with the nuclear briefcase
p. 377 typing in a code

[scene] V.XVI
p. 48 addressing Congress
p. 296 on TV

[scene] V.XVII
p. 123 fighting
p. 339 shot
p. 327 screaming
p. 338 shooting

[scene] V.XVIII

p. 128 flying a plane

p. 94 boarding the Presidential Escape Pod

[scene] V.XIX

p. 346 singing the national anthem

p. 256 lighting a candle in memory of hostages

[scene] V.XX

p. 356 speaking to a crowd with a megaphone

p. 64 at a graveyard

p. 62 at a funeral

[scene] V.XXI

p. 234 in the hospital

p. 395 with a doctor

p. 247 injured

p. 51 addressing the nation on TV

[scene] V.XXII

p. 431 **working out**

p. 117 **drinking water**

[scene] V.XXIII

p. 320 **riding a motorbike**

p. 355 **smoking**

The Lover
[type six]

[scene] VI.I

p. 76 behind his desk in
the Oval Office,
talking to the staff
p. 129 frustrated
p. 427 working late
p. 380 waiting
p. 312 reading files

[scene] VI.II

p. 55 arguing
p. 413 with his wife
p. 327 screaming

[scene] VI.III

p. 351 sitting outside
the Oval Office
p. 105 crying

[scene] VI.IV

p. 342 sick in bed
p. 226 in bed
p. 121 eating in bed
p. 132 getting dressed
p. 266 looking in the mirror
p. 232 in the bathroom

[scene] VI.V

p. 95 briefing staff
p. 183 in a car
p. 158 greeting a crowd

[scene] VI.VI

p. 225 in an elevator
p. 289 on the telephone
p. 60 at a banquet
p. 161 greeting guests at a banquet

[scene] VI.VII

p. 150 giving a speech
p. 106 dancing
p. 113 drinking alcohol

[scene] VI.VIII

p. 57 as a hostage
p. 325 scared
p. 183 in a cable railway
p. 310 praying
p. 169 helpless

[scene] VI.IX

p. 237 in the newspaper

[scene] VI.X

p. 126 fleeing
p. 319 riding a horse

[scene] VI.XI

p. 319 relieved
p. 368 talking to the press
p. 423 with the Secret Service

[scene] VI.XII

p. 268 looking out of the window of the Oval Office

p. 364 talking to his wife

p. 175 hugging his wife

p. 259 looking at a painting

p. 381 walking outside the Oval Office

p. 352 smiling

[scene] VI.XIII

p. 167 having dinner

p. 250 kissing

p. 244 in the shower

p. 275 naked

p. 230 in bed with his wife

[scene] VI.XIV

p. 187 in a church

p. 372 thoughtful

Categories A–W
[Presidents in Illustrations]

Pres.
No.11

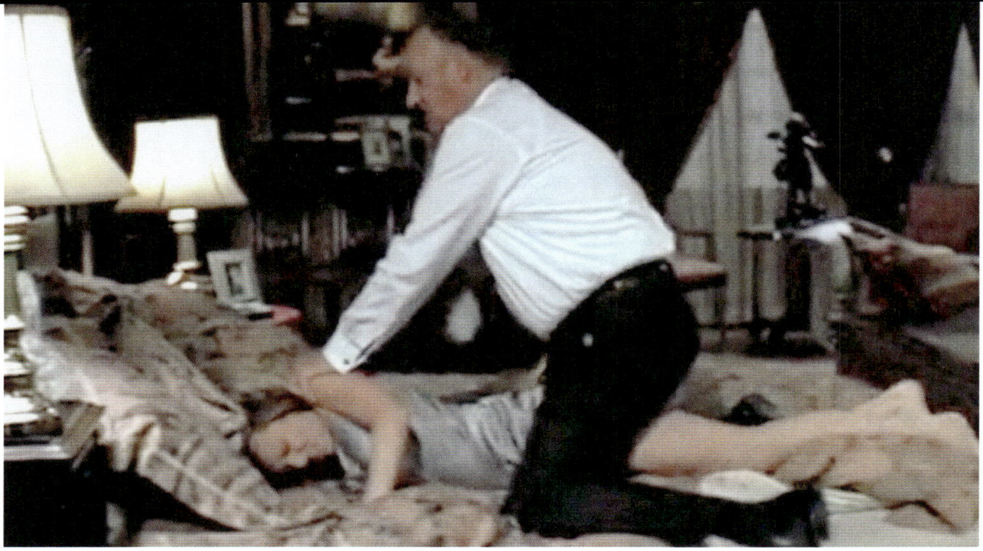

abusing a woman

Pres.
No.34

addressing Congress

Pres.
No.43

Pres.
No.56

Pres.
No.65

Pres.
No.68

Pres.
No.69

Pres.
No.84

Pres.
No.113

Pres.
No.135

Pres.
No.137

Pres.
No.154

Pres.
No.164

Pres. No.1

Pres. No.3

Pres. No.5

Pres.
No.10

Pres.
No.11

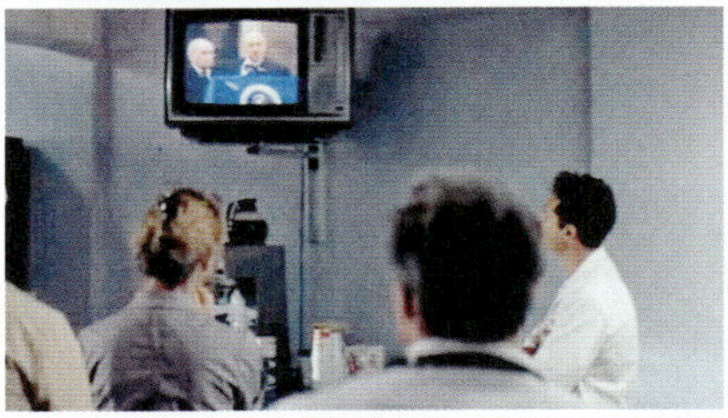

Pres.
No.19

Pres.
No.22

Pres.
No.25

Pres.
No.26

Pres.
No.30

Pres.
No.37

Pres.
No.38

Pres.
No.54

Pres.
No.99

Pres.
No.100

Pres.
No.107

Pres.
No.111

Pres.
No.139

Pres.
No.143

Pres.
No.145

Pres.
No.29

Pres.
No.129

Pres.
No.13

Pres.
No.28

Pres.
No.115

Pres.
No.59

as a DJ

Pres.
No.44

as a hologram

Pres.
No.26

Pres.
No.45

Pres.
No.53

Pres.
No.54

Pres.
No.79

Pres.
No.96

Pres.
No.98

Pres.
No.109

Pres.
No.112

Pres.
No.131

Pres.
No.142

Pres.
No.151

Pres.
No.153

Pres.
No.158

Pres.
No.164

Pres.
No.54

Pres.
No.128

Pres.
No.9

Pres.
No.64

Pres.
No.66

Pres.
No.101

Pres.
No.115

Pres.
No.132

Pres.
No.135

Pres.
No.22

Pres.
No.29

Pres.
No.66

Pres.
No.110

Pres.
No.125

Pres.
No.66

Pres.
No.125

Pres.
No.66

Pres.
No.70

Pres.
No.80

Pres.
No.101

Pres.
No.115

Pres.
No.132

Pres.
No.147

Pres.
No.160

Pres.
No.19

Pres.
No.39

Pres.
No.65

Pres.
No.113

Pres.
No.115

Pres.
No.135

Pres.
No.117

at the United Nations

Pres.
No.21

awarding an officer

Pres.
No.120

Pres.
No.164

Pres.
No.1

Pres.
No.5

Pres.
No.10

Pres.
No.12

Pres.
No.21

Pres.
No.22

Pres.
No.28

Pres.
No.29

Pres.
No.30

Pres.
No.31

Pres.
No.34

Pres.
No.37

Pres.
No.39

Pres.
No.40

Pres.
No.46

Pres.
No.55

Pres.
No.61

Pres.
No.65

Pres.
No.66

Pres.
No.75

Pres.
No.76

Pres.
No.78

Pres.
No.79

Pres.
No.81

Pres.
No.84

Pres.
No.86

Pres.
No.90

Pres.
No.96

Pres.
No.100

Pres.
No.101

Pres.
No.111

Pres.
No.112

Pres.
No.113

Pres.
No.114

Pres.
No.115

Pres.
No.118

Pres.
No.119

Pres.
No.124

Pres.
No.125

Pres.
No.129

Pres.
No.135

Pres.
No.137

Pres.
No.138

Pres.
No.141

Pres.
No.142

Pres.
No.144

Pres.
No.146

Pres.
No.150

Pres.
No.156

Pres.
No.161

Pres.
No.162

Pres.
No.163

Pres.
No.2

Pres.
No.5

Pres.
No.7

behind their desk in the Oval Office, talking to the staff

Pres.
No.11

Pres.
No.12

Pres.
No.22

Pres.
No.26

Pres.
No.29

Pres.
No.30

Pres.
No.31

Pres.
No.39

Pres.
No.47

Pres.
No.49

Pres.
No.50

Pres.
No.53

Pres.
No.55

Pres.
No.67

behind their desk in the Oval Office, talking to the staff

Pres.
No.77

Pres.
No.83

Pres.
No.84

Pres.
No.86

Pres.
No.90

Pres.
No.91

Pres.
No.92

Pres.
No.96

Pres.
No.100

Pres.
No.111

Pres.
No.112

Pres.
No.114

Pres.
No.115

Pres.
No.116

behind their desk in the Oval Office, talking to the staff

Pres.
No.119

Pres.
No.124

Pres.
No.125

Pres.
No.132

Pres.
No.135

Pres.
No.137

Pres.
No.141

Pres.
No.142

Pres.
No.144

Pres.
No.147

Pres.
No.150

Pres.
No.151

Pres.
No.154

Pres.
No.155

behind their desk in the Oval Office, talking to the staff

Pres.
No.156

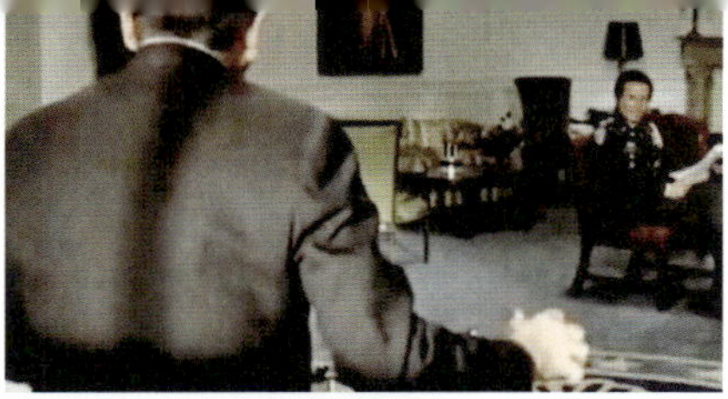

Pres.
No.158

Pres.
No.160

Pres.
No.163

behind their desk in the Oval Office, talking to the staff

Pres.
No.2

Pres.
No.5

Pres.
No.21

Pres.
No.25

Pres.
No.30

Pres.
No.32

Pres.
No.37

Pres.
No.39

Pres.
No.44

Pres.
No.49

Pres.
No.50

Pres.
No.61

Pres.
No.64

Pres.
No.66

Pres.
No.71

Pres.
No.72

Pres.
No.73

Pres.
No.74

Pres.
No.89

Pres.
No.75

Pres.
No.91

Pres.
No.76

Pres.
No.98

Pres.
No.79

Pres.
No.99

Pres.
No.83

Pres.
No.100

Pres.
No.82

Pres.
No.110

Pres.
No.86

Pres.
No.111

Pres.
No.115

Pres.
No.116

Pres.
No.117

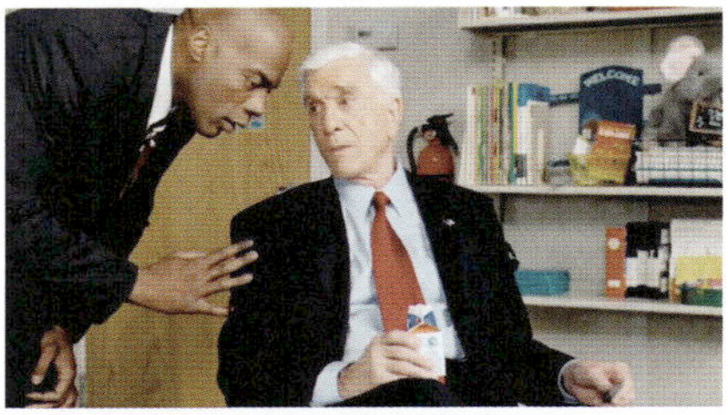

Pres.
No.118

Pres.
No.119

Pres.
No.124

Pres.
No.126

Pres.
No.130

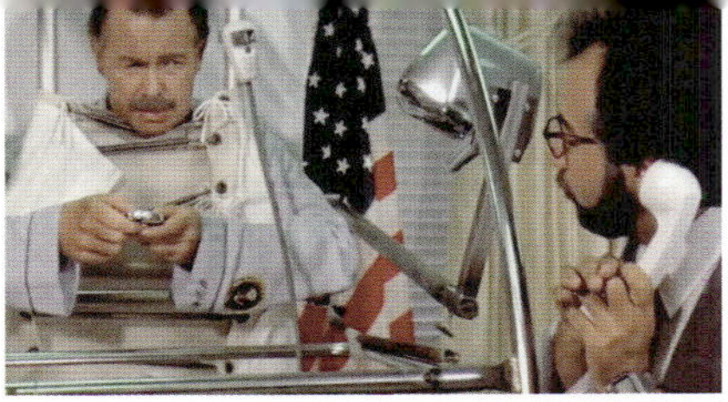

Pres.
No.131

Pres.
No.132

Pres.
No.135

Pres.
No.140

Pres.
No.144

Pres.
No.146

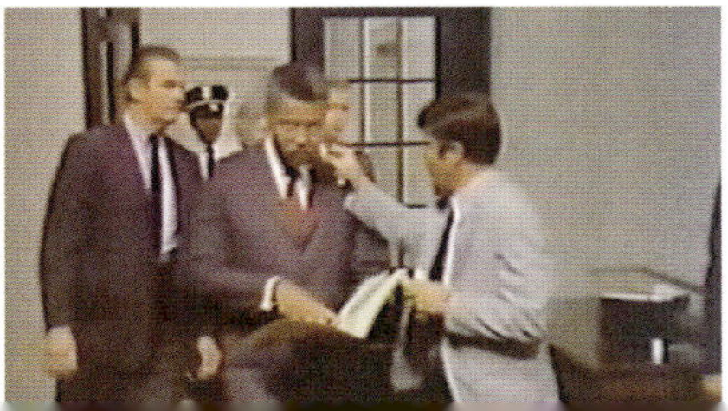

Pres.
No.147

Pres.
No.149

Pres.
No.150

Pres.
No.153

Pres.
No.154

Pres.
No.157

Pres.
No.161

Pres.
No.163

Pres.
No.164

Pres.
No.30

Pres.
No.35

Pres.
No.39

Pres.
No.56

Pres.
No.65

Pres.
No.67

Pres.
No.73

Pres.
No.77

Pres.
No.83

Pres.
No.104

Pres.
No.112

Pres.
No.113

Pres.
No.114

Pres.
No.115

Pres.
No.134

Pres.
No.135

Pres.
No.159

being sworn in

Pres.
No.23

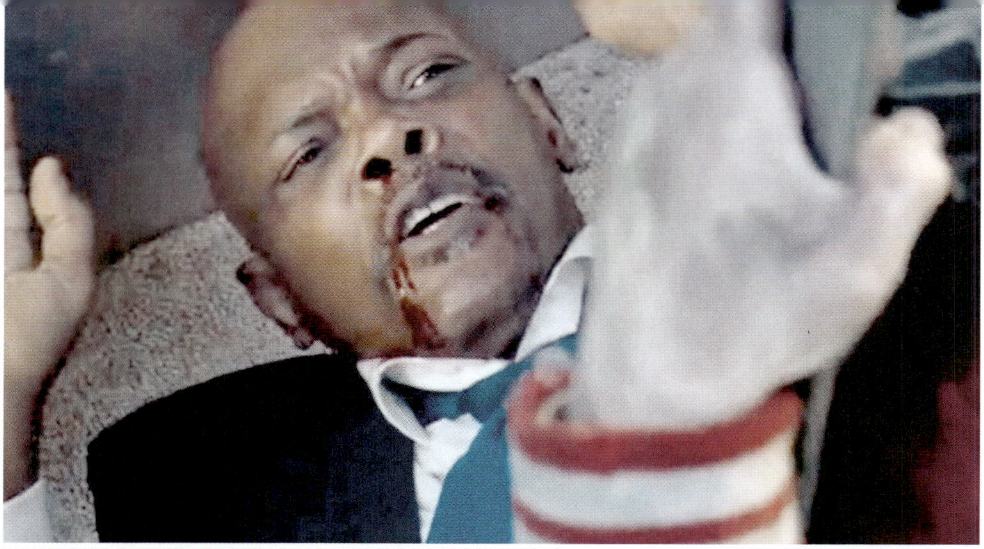

Pres.
No.26

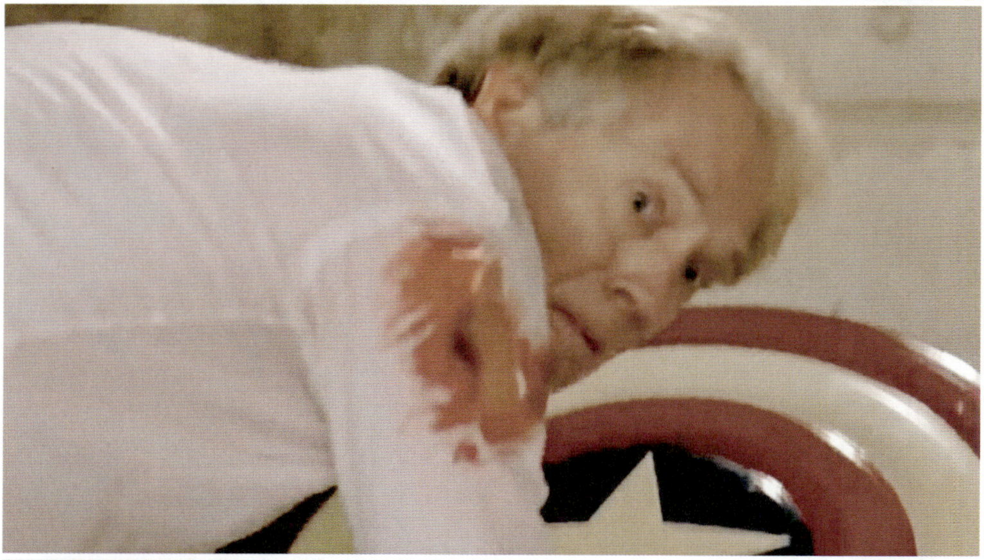

Pres.
No.79

Pres.
No.98

Pres.
No.148

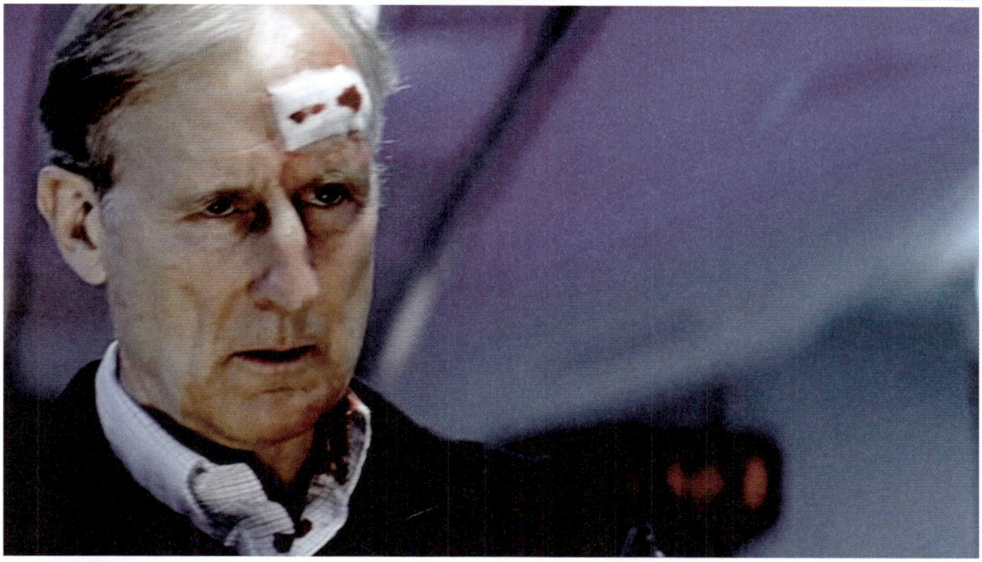

Pres.
No.153

Pres.
No.72

Pres.
No.71

Pres.
No.79

Pres.
No.87

Pres.
No.147

Pres.
No.158

Pres.
No.15

Pres.
No.57

Pres.
No.71

Pres.
No.74

Pres.
No.118

Pres.
No.23

Pres.
No.45

Pres.
No.137

bowling

Pres.
No.4

briefing staff

Pres.
No.10

Pres.
No.13

Pres.
No.15

Pres.
No.30

Pres.
No.46

Pres.
No.48

Pres.
No.52

Pres.
No.90

Pres.
No.98

Pres.
No.100

Pres.
No.104

Pres.
No.107

Pres.
No.108

Pres.
No.111

Pres.
No.117

Pres.
No.118

Pres.
No.126

Pres.
No.129

Pres.
No.140

Pres.
No.144

Pres.
No.148

Pres.
No.149

Pres.
No.154

Pres.
No.155

Pres.
No.156

Pres.
No.161

Pres.
No.1

Pres.
No.4

Pres.
No.5

Pres.
No.10

Pres.
No.29

Pres.
No.30

Pres.
No.37

Pres.
No.39

Pres.
No.41

Pres.
No.44

Pres.
No.61

Pres.
No.65

Pres.
No.82

Pres.
No.84

Pres.
No.86

Pres.
No.100

Pres.
No.106

Pres.
No.108

Pres.
No.110

Pres.
No.111

Pres.
No.112

Pres.
No.114

Pres.
No.118

Pres.
No.119

Pres.
No.130

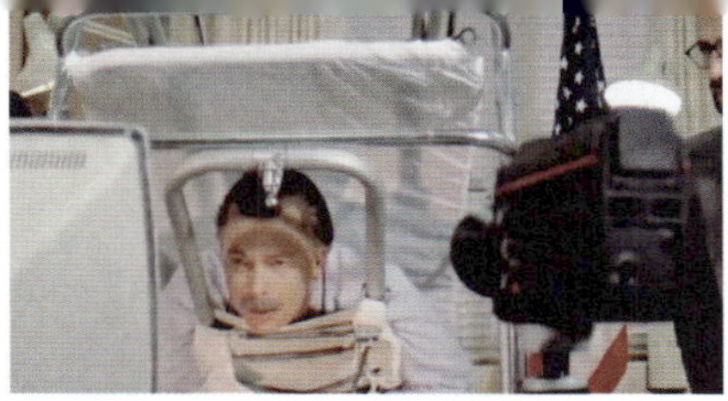

Pres.
No.135

Pres.
No.144

Pres.
No.145

Pres.
No.153

Pres.
No.160

Pres.
No.161

Pres.
No.162

Pres.
No.50

Pres.
No.57

Pres.
No.59

Pres.
No.70

Pres.
No.81

Pres.
No.93

Pres.
No.94

Pres.
No.100

Pres.
No.102

Pres.
No.25

concerned

Pres.
No.1

crying

Pres.
No.50

Pres.
No.54

Pres.
No.59

Pres.
No.100

Pres.
No.102

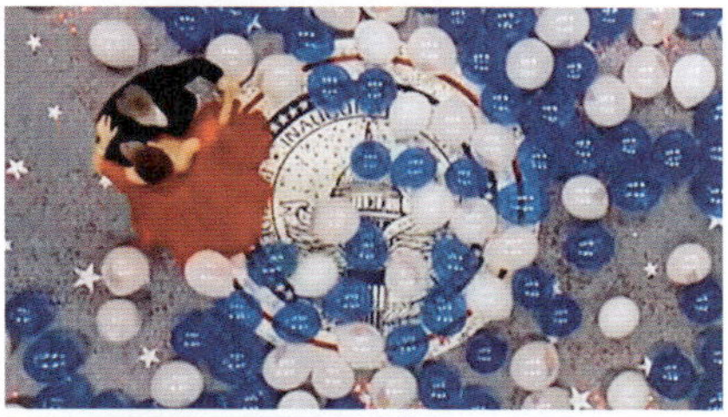

Pres.
No.113

Pres.
No.132

Pres.
No.135

Pres. No.11

Pres. No.56

Pres. No.86

Pres.
No.96

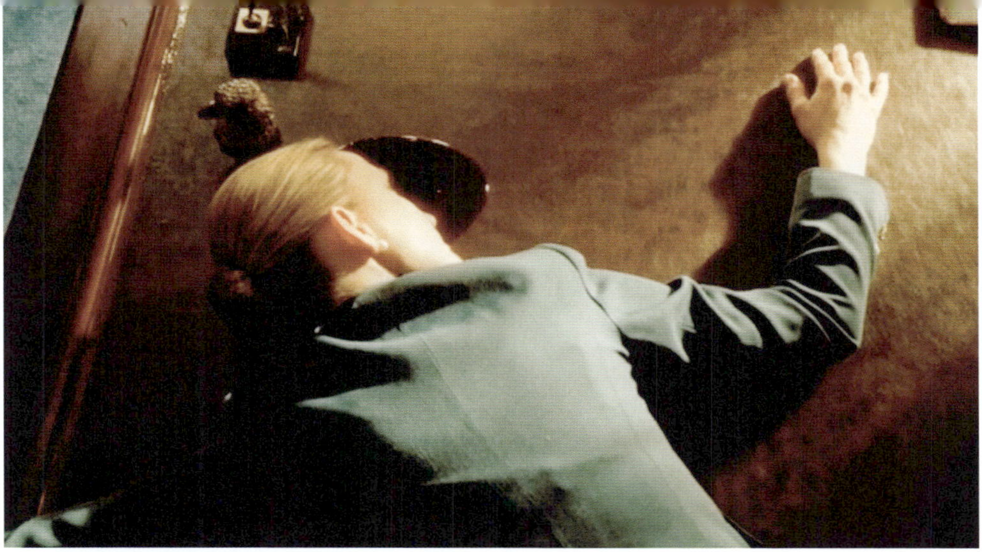

Pres.
No.151

Pres.
No.64

diving

Pres.
No.45

dressed as a woman

Pres.
No.1

Pres.
No.8

Pres.
No.27

Pres.
No.30

Pres.
No.61

Pres.
No.89

Pres.
No.131

Pres.
No.132

Pres.
No.136

Pres.
No.150

Pres.
No.9

Pres.
No.27

Pres.
No.49

Pres.
No.58

Pres.
No.65

Pres.
No.66

Pres.
No.70

Pres.
No.76

Pres.
No.81

Pres.
No.82

Pres.
No.104

Pres.
No.113

Pres.
No.115

Pres.
No.119

Pres.
No.125

Pres.
No.129

Pres.
No.132

Pres.
No.133

Pres.
No.140

Pres.
No.149

Pres.
No.150

Pres.
No.151

Pres.
No.157

Pres.
No.162

Pres.
No.117

drinking milk

Pres.
No.19

drinking through a straw

Pres.
No.25

Pres.
No.61

Pres.
No.117

Pres.
No.119

Pres.
No.149

Pres.
No.160

Pres.
No.23

Pres.
No.34

Pres.
No.137

Pres.
No.144

eating

Pres.
No.50

eating cake

Pres.
No.25

eating chicken wings with another politician

Pres.
No.18

eating in bed

Pres.
No.19

Pres.
No.25

Pres.
No.9

Pres.
No.15

Pres.
No.23

Pres.
No.26

Pres.
No.53

Pres.
No.110

Pres.
No.116

Pres.
No.131

Pres.
No.162

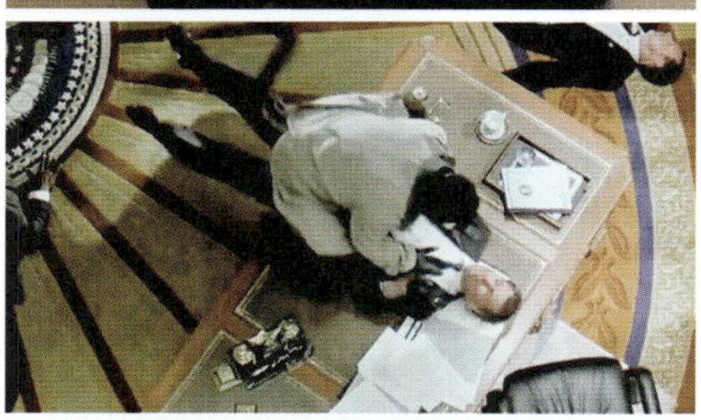

Pres.
No.164

Pres.
No.64

fighting with a lightsaber

Pres.
No.9

fishing

Pres.
No.26

Pres.
No.61

Pres.
No.70

Pres.
No.71

Pres.
No.72

Pres.
No.79

Pres.
No.87

Pres.
No.101

Pres.
No.106

Pres.
No.110

Pres.
No.116

Pres.
No.128

Pres.
No.131

Pres.
No.147

Pres.
No.148

Pres.
No.158

Pres.
No.162

Pres.
No.14

Pres.
No.15

Pres.
No.71

Pres.
No.1

Pres.
No.25

Pres.
No.30

Pres.
No.34

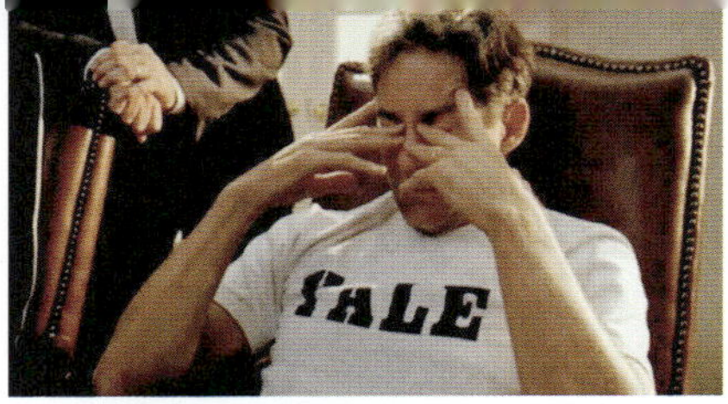

Pres.
No.86

Pres.
No.92

Pres.
No.99

Pres.
No.100

Pres.
No.111

Pres. No.13

Pres. No.90

Pres. No.129

Pres.
No.28

getting a promise from his daughter

Pres.
No.9

getting dressed

Pres.
No.83

Pres.
No.94

Pres.
No.98

Pres.
No.115

Pres.
No.132

Pres.
No.19

getting his nose licked

Pres.
No.34

getting into a car

Pres.
No.79

Pres.
No.116

Pres.
No.128

Pres. No.148

Pres. No.153

Pres. No.158

Pres.
No.33

Pres.
No.57

Pres.
No.61

Pres.
No.64

Pres.
No.71

Pres.
No.72

Pres.
No.79

Pres.
No.113

Pres.
No.158

Pres.
No.160

Pres.
No.70

Pres.
No.79

Pres.
No.128

getting out of Air Force One

Pres.
No.129

Pres.
No.142

Pres.
No.151

Pres.
No.15

Pres.
No.89

Pres.
No.101

Pres.
No.18

Pres.
No.25

Pres.
No.30

Pres.
No.39

Pres.
No.50

Pres.
No.56

Pres.
No.57

Pres.
No.61

Pres.
No.70

Pres.
No.79

Pres.
No.80

Pres.
No.82

Pres.
No.87

Pres.
No.89

Pres.
No.104

Pres.
No.127

Pres.
No.131

Pres.
No.142

Pres.
No.147

Pres.
No.153

Pres.
No.157

Pres.
No.161

Pres.
No.164

Pres.
No.5

Pres.
No.9

Pres.
No.11

Pres. No.28

Pres. No.29

Pres. No.30

Pres.
No.34

Pres.
No.37

Pres.
No.40

Pres.
No.50

Pres.
No.65

Pres.
No.66

Pres.
No.67

Pres.
No.71

Pres.
No.74

Pres.
No.80

Pres.
No.86

Pres.
No.98

Pres.
No.104

Pres.
No.108

Pres.
No.125

Pres.
No.132

Pres.
No.134

Pres.
No.135

Pres.
No.146

Pres.
No.147

Pres.
No.160

Pres.
No.4

Pres.
No.11

Pres.
No.12

Pres. No.15

Pres. No.22

Pres. No.25

Pres. No.31

Pres. No.32

Pres. No.34

Pres. No.33

Pres. No.36

Pres. No.37

Pres. No.39

Pres. No.43

Pres. No.44

Pres. No.45

Pres. No.50

Pres.
No.52

Pres.
No.53

Pres.
No.54

Pres.
No.56

Pres.
No.57

Pres.
No.58

Pres.
No.59

Pres.
No.62

Pres.
No.63

Pres.
No.64

Pres.
No.65

Pres.
No.66

Pres.
No.67

Pres.
No.69

Pres.
No.70

Pres.
No.72

Pres.
No.84

Pres.
No.92

Pres.
No.93

Pres.
No.94

Pres.
No.95

Pres.
No.98

Pres.
No.102

Pres.
No.104

Pres.
No.106

Pres.
No.107

Pres.
No.108

Pres.
No.109

Pres.
No.110

Pres.
No.115

Pres.
No.116

Pres.
No.119

Pres.
No.120

Pres.
No.121

Pres.
No.125

Pres.
No.127

Pres.
No.128

Pres.
No.129

Pres.
No.131

Pres.
No.135

Pres.
No.137

Pres.
No.145

Pres.
No.146

Pres.
No.147

Pres.
No.148

Pres.
No.150

Pres.
No.152

Pres.
No.153

Pres.
No.155

Pres.
No.157

Pres.
No.160

Pres.
No.161

Pres.
No.117

giving a speech at the United Nations naked

Pres.
No.9

giving an interview with his wife

Pres.
No.58

Pres.
No.68

Pres.
No.69

Pres.
No.2

Pres.
No.34

Pres.
No.43

Pres.
No.64

Pres.
No.137

Pres.
No.70

Pres.
No.142

Pres.
No.95

Pres.
No.147

Pres.
No.104

Pres.
No.153

Pres.
No.121

Pres.
No.154

Pres.
No.128

Pres.
No.164

Pres.
No.132

Pres.
No.34

Pres.
No.149

Pres.
No.28

Pres.
No.50

Pres.
No.56

greeting guests at a banquet

Pres. No.70

Pres. No.132

Pres. No.137

greeting guests at a banquet

Pres.
No.15

Pres.
No.29

Pres.
No.151

Pres.
No.135

hanging a picture in the Oval Office

Pres.
No.9

having breakfast

Pres.
No.28

Pres.
No.30

Pres.
No.53

Pres.
No.71

Pres.
No.92

Pres.
No.157

Pres.
No.9

Pres.
No.34

Pres.
No.53

Pres.
No.86

Pres.
No.125

Pres.
No.132

Pres.
No.1

Pres.
No.5

Pres.
No.48

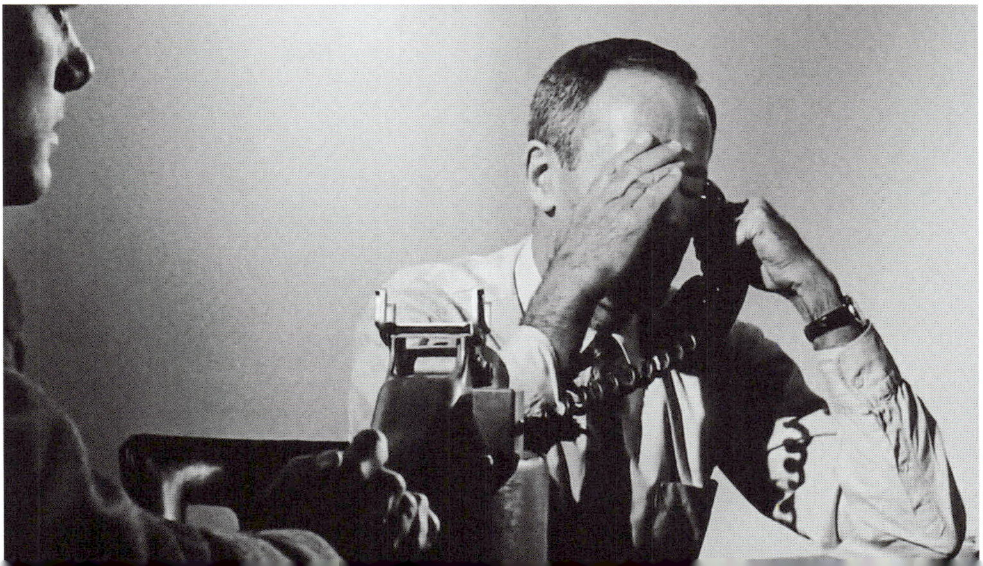

Pres.
No.51

Pres.
No.78

Pres.
No.99

Pres.
No.116

Pres.
No.148

Pres.
No.15

Pres.
No.20

Pres.
No.26

Pres.
No.44

Pres.
No.45

Pres.
No.53

Pres.
No.66

Pres.
No.70

Pres.
No.74

Pres.
No.76

Pres.
No.79

Pres.
No.87

Pres.
No.101

Pres.
No.110

Pres.
No.162

Pres.
No.1

his wife holding his face

Pres.
No.18

holding up a dog's ears

Pres.
No.107

hugging her son

Pres.
No.15

hugging his family

Pres.
No.1

Pres.
No.4

Pres.
No.14

hugging his wife

Pres.
No.39

Pres.
No.92

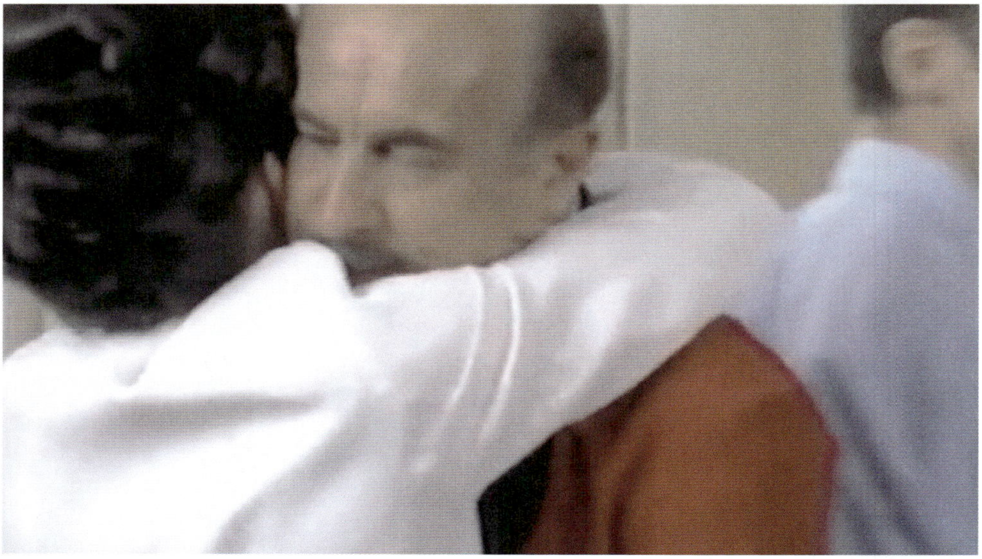

Pres.
No.131

hugging his wife

Pres.
No.9

Pres.
No.28

Pres.
No.30

hugging their daughter

Pres.
No.31

Pres.
No.51

Pres.
No.71

Pres.
No.92

Pres.
No.12

Pres.
No.31

Pres.
No.56

Pres.
No.66

Pres.
No.71

Pres.
No.119

Pres.
No.135

Pres.
No.160

Pres.
No.110

Pres.
No.111

Pres.
No.120

Pres.
No.148

Pres.
No.151

Pres.
No.158

Pres.
No.53

in a cable railway

Pres.
No.8

in a car

Pres.
No.34

Pres.
No.56

Pres.
No.57

Pres.
No.58

Pres.
No.63

Pres.
No.70

Pres.
No.76

Pres.
No.79

Pres.
No.84

Pres.
No.89

Pres.
No.92

Pres.
No.94

Pres.
No.97

Pres.
No.98

Pres.
No.101

Pres.
No.102

Pres.
No.125

Pres.
No.126

Pres.
No.131

Pres.
No.132

Pres.
No.142

Pres.
No.147

Pres.
No.148

Pres.
No.151

Pres.
No.153

Pres.
No.157

Pres.
No.158

Pres.
No.160

Pres.
No.10

Pres.
No.59

Pres.
No.44

Pres.
No.110

Pres.
No.144

Pres.
No.148

Pres.
No.161

Pres.
No.3

Pres.
No.8

Pres.
No.9

Pres.
No.12

Pres.
No.17

Pres.
No.19

Pres.
No.22

Pres.
No.29

Pres.
No.30

Pres.
No.39

Pres.
No.42

Pres.
No.44

Pres.
No.47

Pres.
No.48

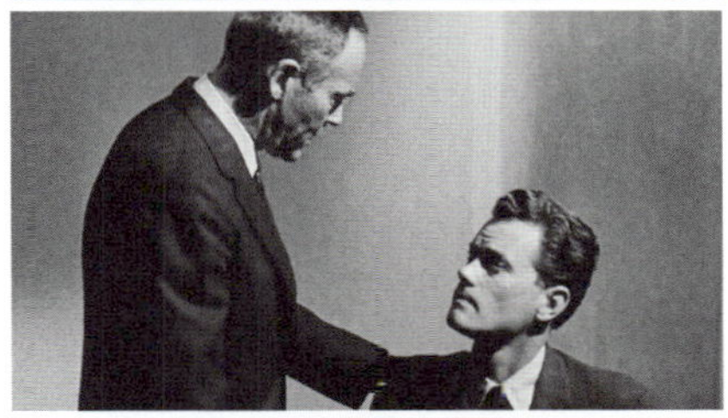

Pres.
No.56

Pres.
No.59

Pres.
No.61

Pres. No.64

Pres. No.65

Pres. No.66

Pres. No.71

Pres. No.73

Pres. No.76

Pres. No.80

Pres. No.82

Pres. No.83

Pres. No.84

Pres. No.91

Pres. No.95

Pres. No.96

Pres. No.98

Pres.
No.100

Pres.
No.101

Pres.
No.103

Pres.
No.104

Pres.
No.105

Pres.
No.107

Pres.
No.108

Pres.
No.110

Pres.
No.111

Pres.
No.112

Pres.
No.113

Pres.
No.114

Pres.
No.115

Pres.
No.116

Pres.
No.119

Pres.
No.124

Pres.
No.125

Pres.
No.126

Pres.
No.128

Pres.
No.129

Pres.
No.131

Pres.
No.132

Pres.
No.133

Pres.
No.136

Pres.
No.140

Pres.
No.142

Pres.
No.144

Pres.
No.147

Pres.
No.149

Pres.
No.150

Pres.
No.151

Pres.
No.157

Pres.
No.158

Pres.
No.161

Pres.
No.163

Pres.
No.164

Pres.
No.5

Pres.
No.25

Pres.
No.39

Pres.
No.57

Pres.
No.130

Pres.
No.148

Pres.
No.23

in a floating fridge

Pres.
No.61

in a helicopter

Pres.
No.79

Pres.
No.87

Pres.
No.93

Pres.
No.147

Pres.
No.158

Pres.
No.161

Pres.
No.34

Pres.
No.59

Pres.
No.71

in a lab

Pres.
No.1

in a meeting

Pres.
No.2

Pres.
No.3

Pres.
No.6

Pres. No.7

Pres. No.9

Pres. No.13

Pres. No.16

Pres. No.19

Pres. No.20

Pres. No.21

Pres. No.25

Pres. No.27

Pres. No.29

Pres. No.30

Pres. No.33

Pres. No.34

Pres. No.39

Pres.
No.42

Pres.
No.48

Pres.
No.49

Pres.
No.50

Pres.
No.56

Pres.
No.57

Pres.
No.66

Pres.
No.71

Pres.
No.74

Pres.
No.75

Pres.
No.80

Pres.
No.82

Pres.
No.83

Pres.
No.86

Pres.
No.87

Pres.
No.99

Pres.
No.100

Pres.
No.110

Pres.
No.112

Pres.
No.114

Pres.
No.115

Pres.
No.119

Pres.
No.126

Pres.
No.128

Pres.
No.129

Pres.
No.132

Pres.
No.135

Pres.
No.136

Pres.
No.138

Pres.
No.145

Pres.
No.146

Pres.
No.148

Pres.
No.150

Pres.
No.161

Pres.
No.163

Pres.
No.30

Pres.
No.39

Pres.
No.65

Pres.
No.66

Pres.
No.68

Pres.
No.71

Pres.
No.76

Pres.
No.77

Pres.
No.82

Pres.
No.83

Pres.
No.90

Pres.
No.91

Pres.
No.96

Pres.
No.98

Pres.
No.100

Pres.
No.111

Pres.
No.114

Pres.
No.115

Pres.
No.124

Pres.
No.125

Pres.
No.129

Pres.
No.132

Pres.
No.135

Pres.
No.137

Pres.
No.142

Pres.
No.146

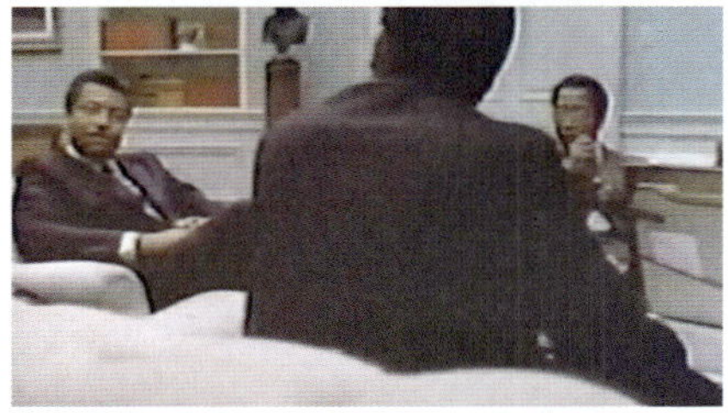

Pres.
No.147

Pres.
No.150

Pres.
No.151

Pres.
No.154

Pres.
No.155

Pres.
No.156

Pres.
No.160

Pres.
No.162

Pres.
No.164

Pres.
No.2

Pres.
No.6

Pres.
No.25

Pres.
No.48

Pres.
No.107

Pres.
No.145

Pres.
No.9

Pres.
No.5

Pres.
No.20

Pres.
No.21

Pres.
No.42

Pres.
No.54

Pres.
No.86

Pres.
No.111

Pres.
No.124

Pres.
No.144

Pres.
No.154

Pres.
No.37

Pres.
No.70

Pres.
No.84

Pres.
No.104

Pres.
No.131

Pres.
No.147

Pres. No.31

Pres. No.117

Pres.
No.27

Pres.
No.137

Pres.
No.157

Pres.
No.161

in a tracksuit

Pres.
No.2

in a video conference

Pres.
No.3

Pres.
No.4

Pres.
No.10

Pres.
No.13

Pres.
No.20

Pres.
No.21

Pres.
No.57

Pres.
No.71

Pres.
No.72

Pres.
No.79

Pres.
No.88

Pres.
No.119

Pres.
No.123

Pres.
No.128

Pres.
No.136

Pres.
No.163

Pres.
No.39

Pres.
No.51

Pres.
No.74

Pres. No.79

Pres. No.98

in a video conference with a terrorist

Pres. No.110

Pres. No.120

Pres. No.131

Pres.
No.135

in an elevator

Pres.
No.9

in bed

Pres.
No.18

Pres.
No.56

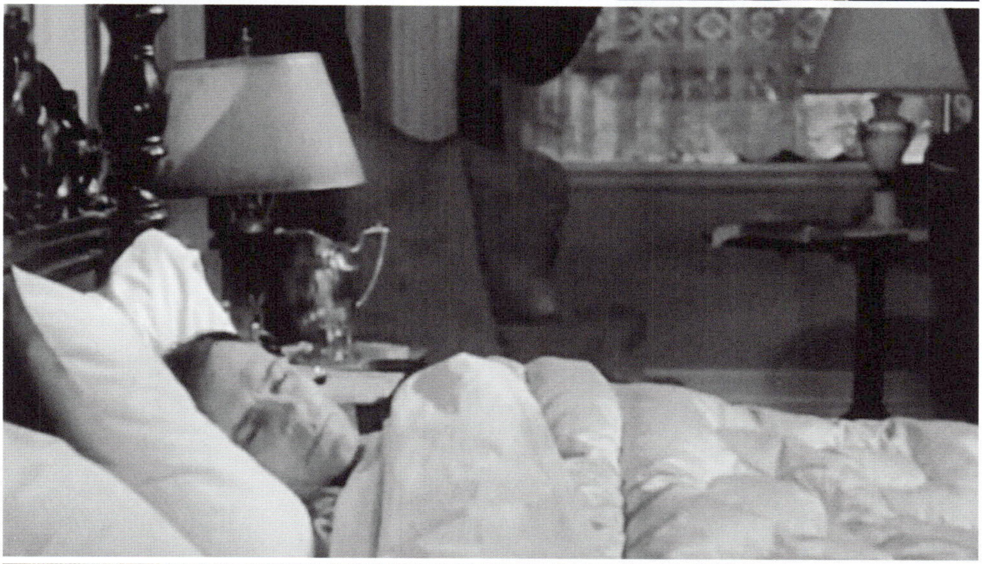

Pres.
No.59

Pres.
No.66

Pres.
No.93

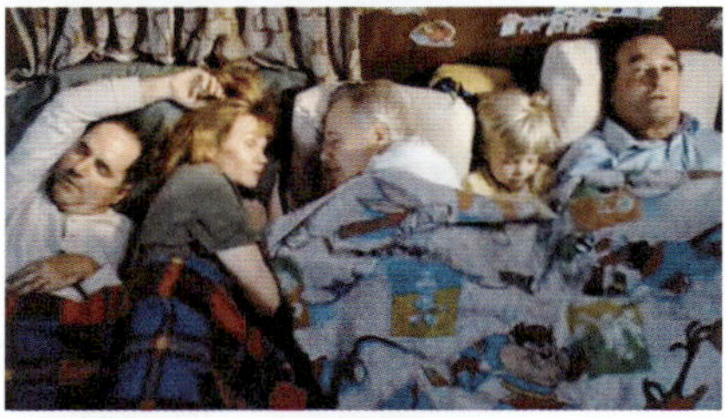

Pres.
No.117

Pres.
No.130

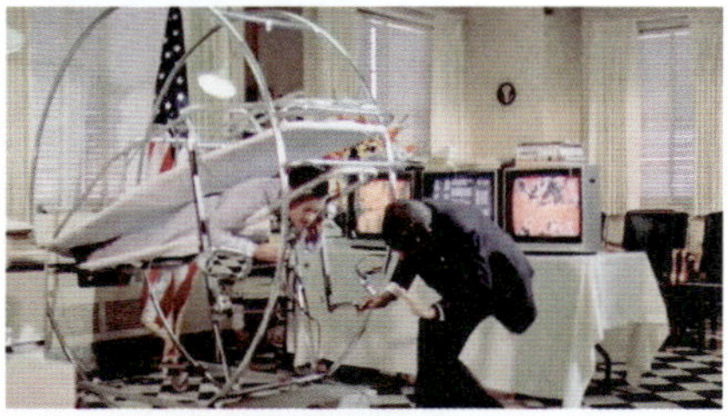

Pres.
No.132

Pres.
No.160

Pres.
No.30

in bed with her husband

Pres.
No.19

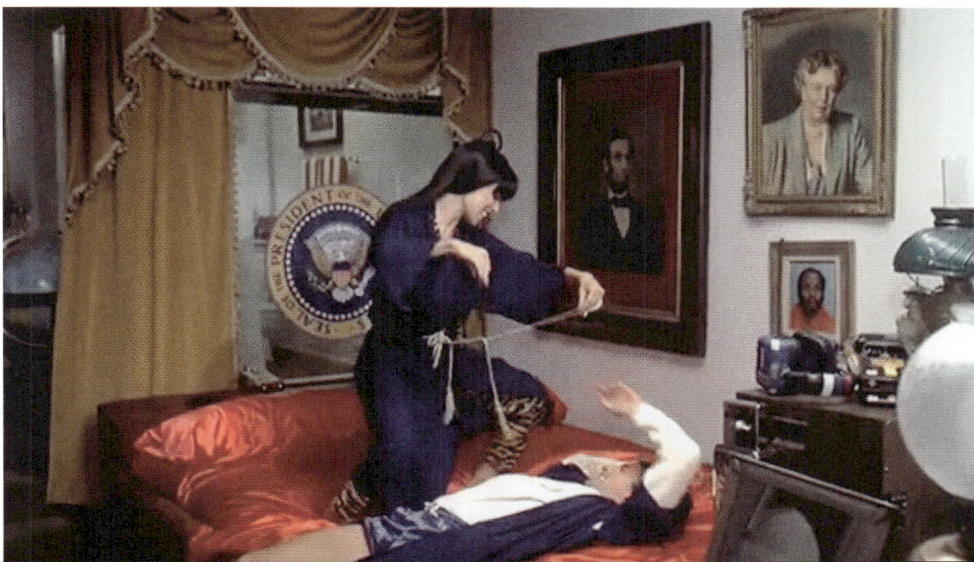

in bed with his mistress

Pres.
No.9

Pres.
No.18

Pres.
No.19

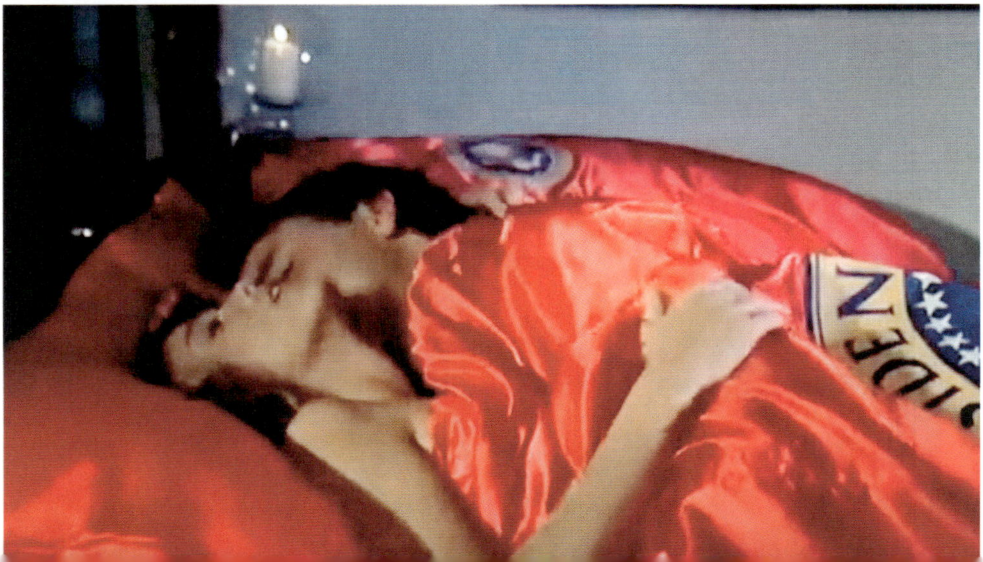

Pres.
No.22

Pres.
No.86

Pres.
No.105

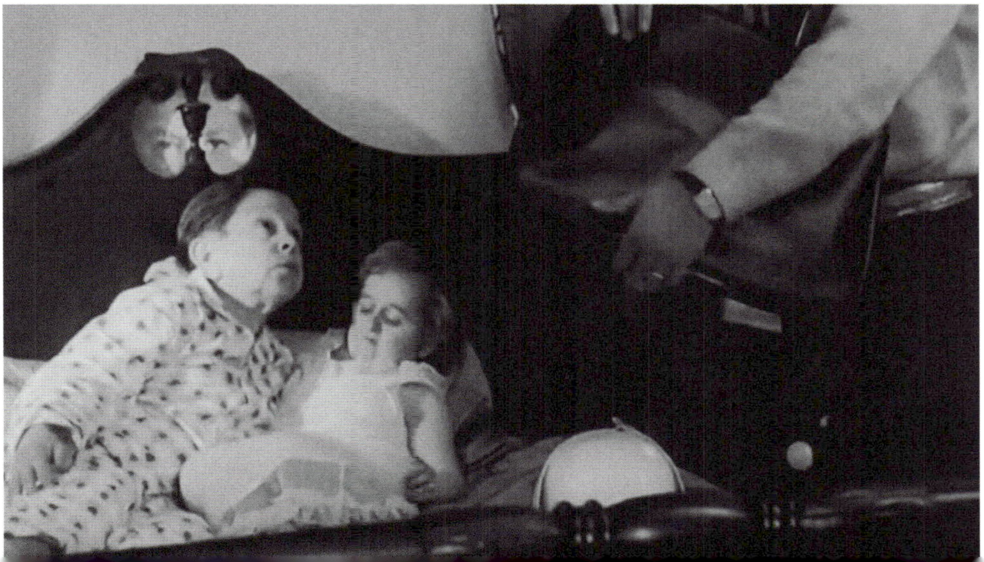

Pres.
No.135

in bed with his wife

Pres.
No.94

in the bathroom

Pres.
No.102

in the bathroom

Pres.
No.23

in the crashed Air Force One

Pres.
No.33

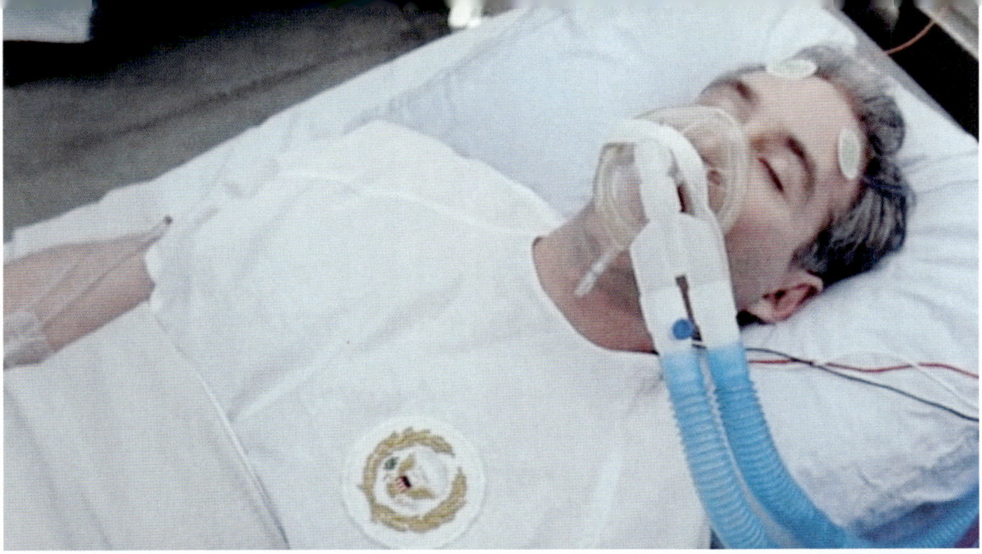

Pres.
No.39

Pres.
No.49

Pres.
No.52

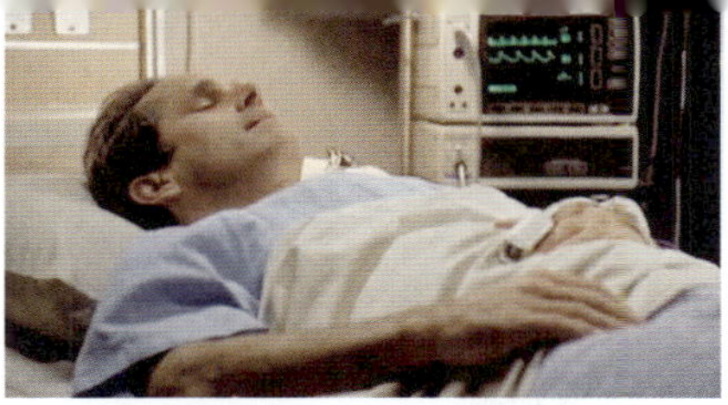

Pres.
No.63

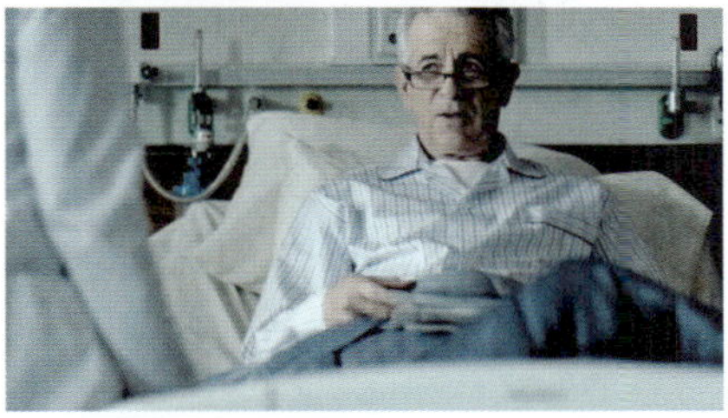

Pres.
No.111

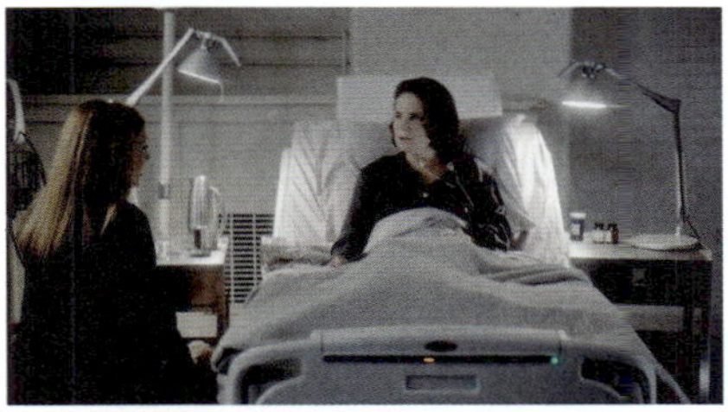

Pres.
No.113

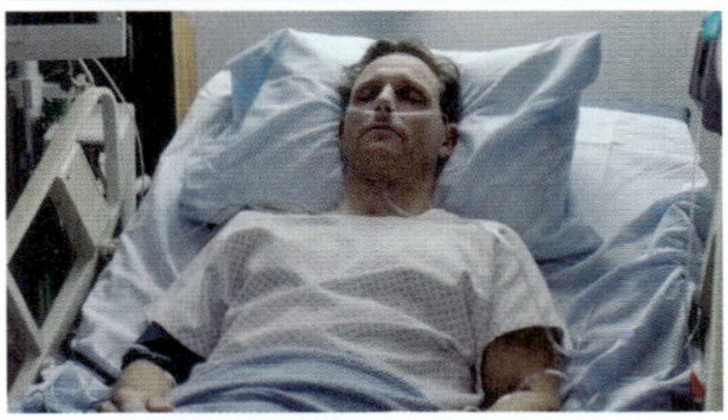

Pres.
No.149

Pres.
No.34

Pres.
No.60

Pres.
No.66

Pres. No.19

Pres. No.23

Pres. No.25

Pres. No.26

Pres. No.52

Pres. No.66

Pres. No.70

Pres. No.84

Pres. No.135

Pres.
No.3

Pres.
No.15

Pres.
No.23

in the office on board Air Force One

Pres. No.128

Pres. No.129

Pres. No.142

in the office on board Air Force One

Pres.
No.5

Pres.
No.12

Pres.
No.21

in the Oval Office talking to the staff

Pres.
No.52

Pres.
No.53

Pres.
No.55

Pres.
No.56

Pres.
No.65

Pres.
No.68

Pres.
No.71

Pres.
No.77

Pres.
No.79

Pres.
No.83

Pres.
No.112

Pres.
No.113

Pres.
No.114

Pres.
No.124

Pres.
No.125

Pres.
No.132

Pres.
No.135

Pres.
No.142

Pres.
No.150

Pres.
No.164

Pres.
No.34

in the shower

Pres.
No.6

in the Situation Room

Pres. No.37

Pres. No.39

Pres. No.40

Pres.
No.55

Pres.
No.67

Pres.
No.82

Pres.
No.100

Pres.
No.114

Pres.
No.140

Pres.
No.149

Pres.
No.20

incredulous

Pres.
No.23

injured

Pres.
No.24

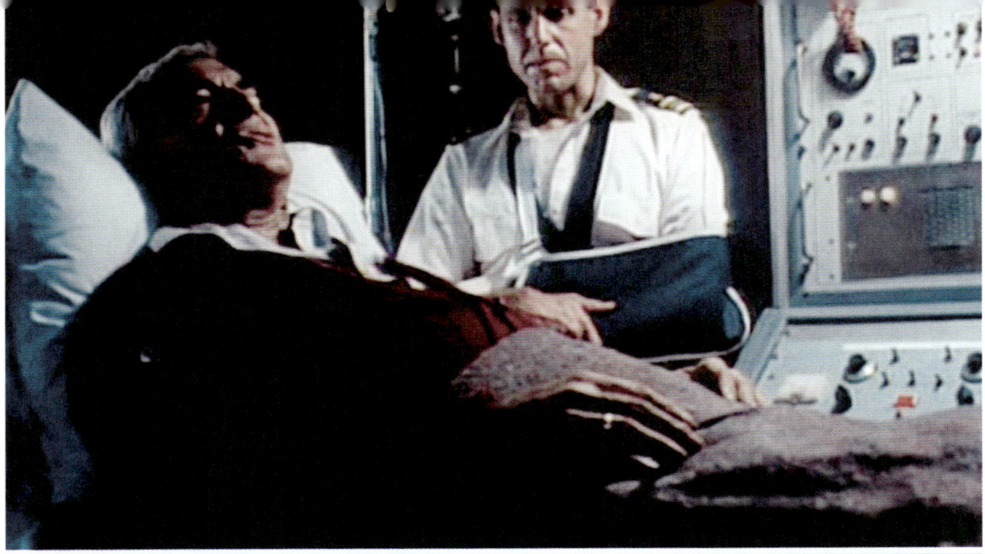

Pres.
No.39

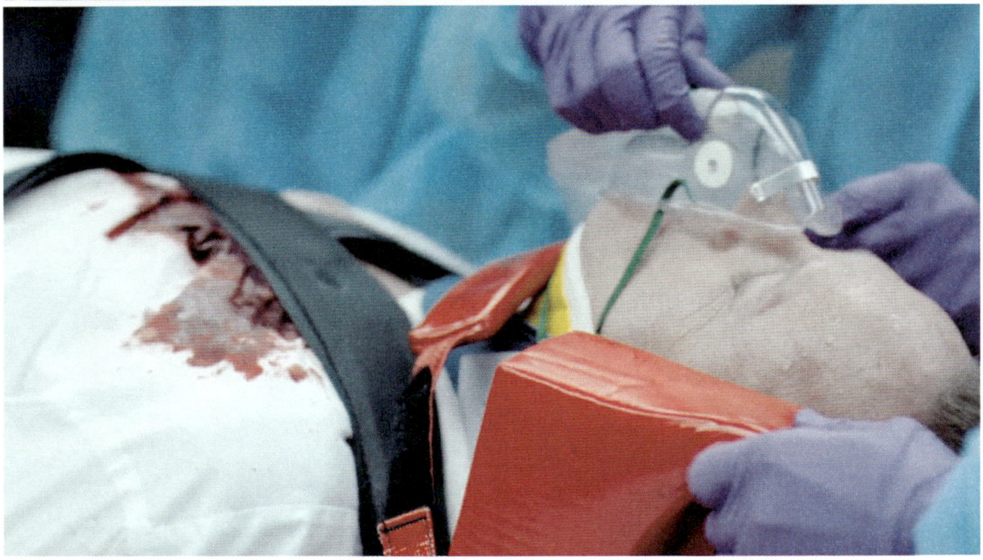

Pres.
No.56

injured

Pres.
No.97

Pres.
No.98

Pres.
No.109

Pres.
No.113

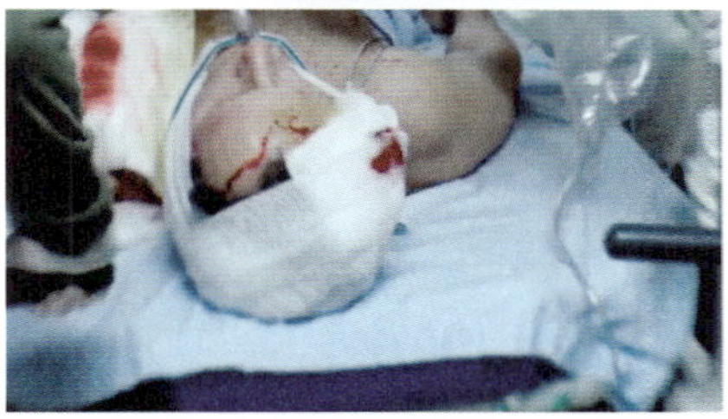

Pres.
No.120

Pres.
No.148

Pres.
No.153

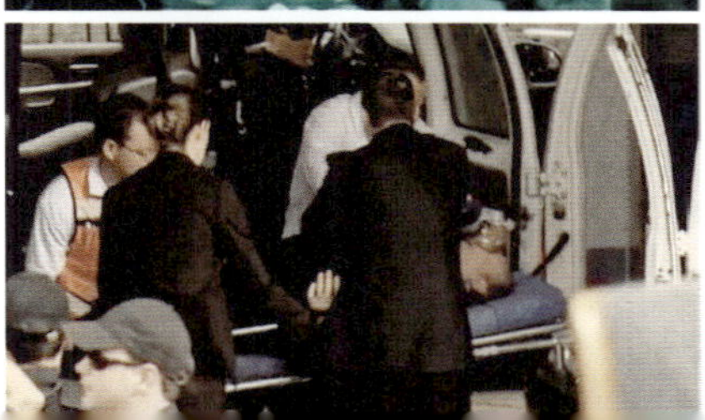

Pres.
No.158

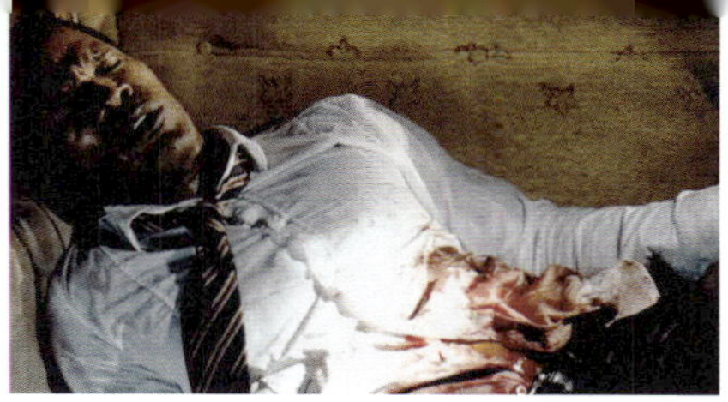

Pres.
No.11

killing

Pres.
No.9

kissing

Pres.
No.15

Pres.
No.19

Pres.
No.30

Pres.
No.59

Pres.
No.71

Pres.
No.75

Pres.
No.98

Pres.
No.105

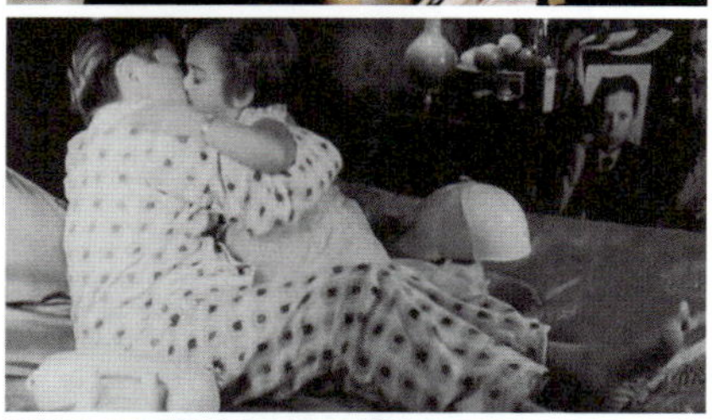

Pres.
No.131

Pres.
No.132

Pres.
No.135

Pres.
No.141

Pres.
No.11

Pres.
No.113

Pres.
No.20

Pres.
No.25

Pres.
No.133

Pres. No.18

Pres. No.19

Pres.
No.32

lighting a candle in memory of hostages

Pres.
No.116

listening to music

Pres.
No.26

Pres.
No.87

Pres.
No.92

Pres.
No.96

locked up

Pres.
No.64

looking at a globe

Pres.
No.89

Pres.
No.116

Pres.
No.6

Pres.
No.30

Pres.
No.32

Pres.
No.39

Pres.
No.161

Pres.
No.72

Pres.
No.99

Pres.
No.98

Pres.
No.114

Pres.
No.144

Pres.
No.149

Pres.
No.71

looking at a spaceship

Pres.
No.18

looking at memories

Pres.
No.34

looking at memories

Pres.
No.21

looking at military strategies

Pres.
No.37

Pres.
No.71

Pres.
No.76

Pres.
No.87

Pres.
No.118

Pres.
No.126

Pres.
No.144

Pres.
No.156

Pres.
No.161

Pres.
No.58

Pres.
No.59

Pres.
No.124

Pres.
No.129

Pres.
No.130

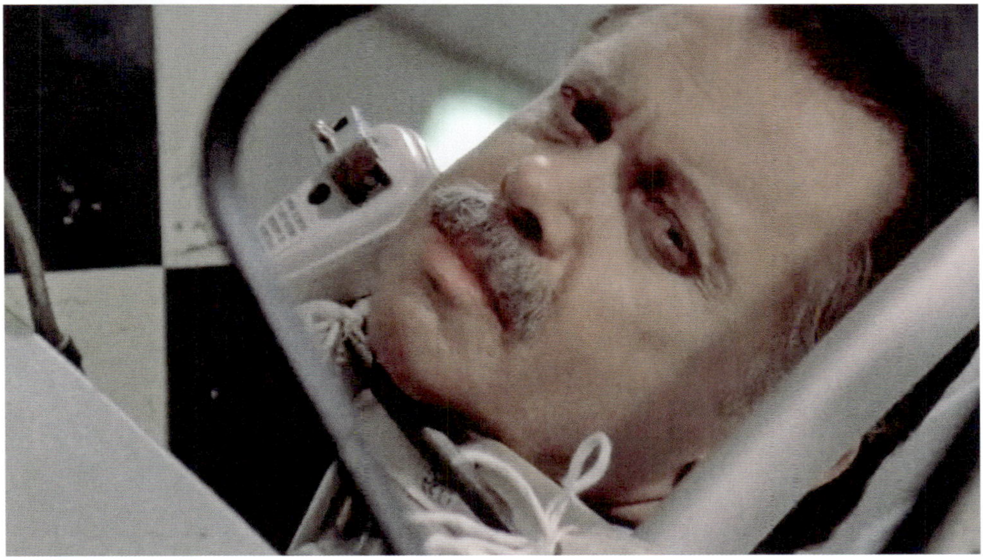

Pres.
No.7

Pres.
No.9

Pres.
No.11

Pres.
No.12

Pres.
No.46

Pres.
No.55

Pres.
No.66

Pres.
No.79

Pres.
No.113

Pres.
No.116

Pres.
No.118

Pres.
No.135

Pres.
No.142

Pres.
No.145

Pres.
No.151

Pres.
No.162

Pres.
No.5

Pres.
No.13

Pres.
No.44

Pres.
No.51

Pres.
No.57

Pres.
No.72

Pres.
No.76

Pres.
No.87

Pres.
No.99

Pres.
No.115

Pres.
No.118

Pres.
No.144

Pres.
No.163

Pres.
No.137

making smoke rings

Pres.
No.10

meeting another politician

Pres.
No.18

Pres.
No.21

Pres.
No.25

meeting another politician

Pres.
No.54

Pres.
No.66

Pres.
No.80

Pres.
No.98

Pres.
No.115

Pres.
No.137

Pres.
No.147

Pres.
No.149

Pres.
No.153

Pres.
No.117

naked

Pres.
No.64

offering candies

Pres.
No.39

Pres.
No.154

Pres.
No.158

on a phone screen

Pres.
No.50

Pres.
No.74

Pres.
No.92

on a sign

Pres.
No.104

on a sign

Pres.
No.32

on a stage

Pres.
No.50

Pres.
No.59

Pres.
No.85

Pres.
No.129

Pres.
No.153

Pres.
No.23

on a tin can telephone

Pres.
No.15

on board Air Force One

Pres.
No.27

Pres.
No.64

Pres.
No.71

Pres.
No.84

Pres.
No.88

Pres.
No.93

Pres.
No.94

Pres.
No.128

Pres.
No.129

Pres.
No.142

Pres.
No.148

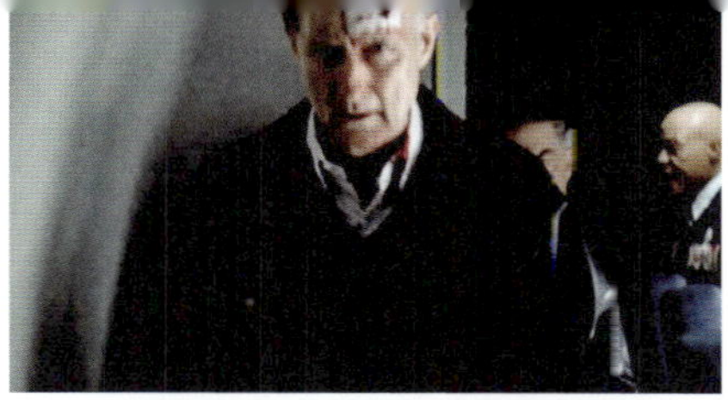

Pres.
No.157

Pres.
No.144

on board a ship

Pres.
No.10

on the cell phone

Pres.
No.15

Pres.
No.26

Pres.
No.53

Pres.
No.61

Pres.
No.74

Pres.
No.84

Pres.
No.104

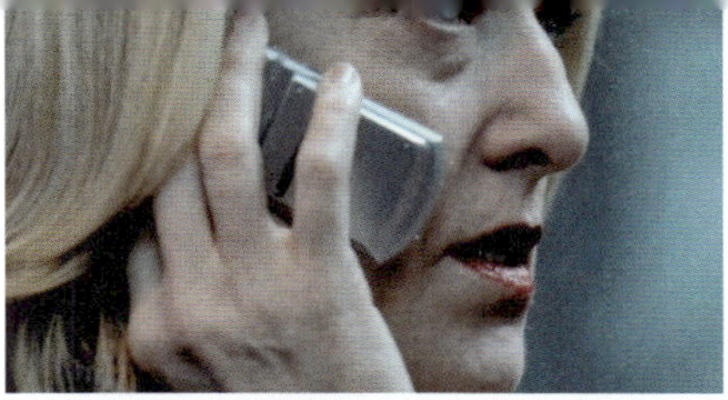

Pres.
No.131

Pres.
No.140

Pres.
No.153

Pres.
No.158

Pres.
No.25

Pres.
No.86

Pres.
No.156

Pres.
No.1

Pres.
No.2

Pres.
No.3

Pres.
No.7

Pres.
No.12

Pres.
No.15

Pres.
No.22

Pres.
No.24

Pres.
No.25

Pres.
No.26

Pres.
No.27

Pres.
No.28

Pres.
No.30

Pres.
No.34

Pres.
No.41

Pres.
No.42

Pres.
No.46

Pres.
No.47

Pres.
No.48

Pres.
No.50

Pres.
No.51

Pres.
No.52

Pres.
No.53

Pres.
No.59

Pres.
No.66

Pres.
No.71

Pres.
No.76

Pres.
No.77

Pres.
No.79

Pres.
No.84

Pres.
No.91

Pres.
No.94

Pres.
No.96

Pres.
No.101

Pres.
No.105

Pres.
No.110

Pres.
No.114

Pres.
No.119

Pres.
No.126

Pres.
No.129

Pres.
No.132

Pres.
No.136

Pres.
No.138

Pres.
No.140

Pres.
No.142

Pres.
No.148

Pres.
No.151

Pres.
No.153

Pres.
No.156

Pres.
No.157

Pres.
No.160

Pres.
No.161

Pres.
No.22

Pres.
No.105

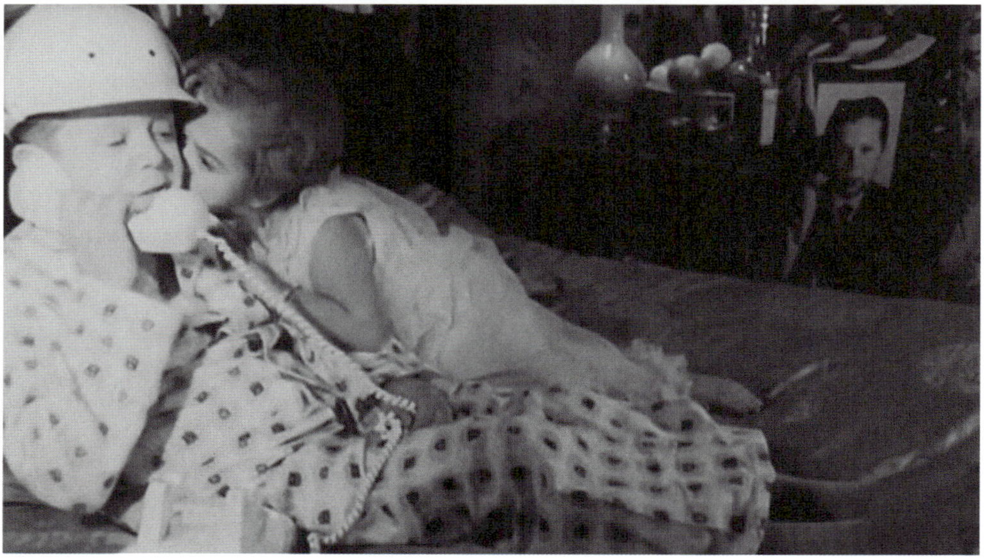

on the telephone, looking at files

Pres.
No.1

Pres.
No.7

Pres.
No.28

Pres.
No.9

Pres.
No.2

Pres.
No.11

Pres. No.13

Pres. No.18

Pres. No.22

Pres. No.25

Pres. No.28

Pres. No.29

Pres. No.30

Pres. No.34

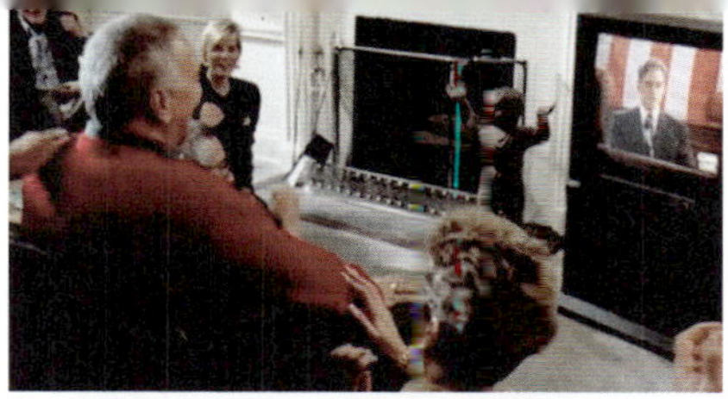

Pres. No.33

Pres. No.37

Pres. No.38

Pres. No.39

Pres. No.40

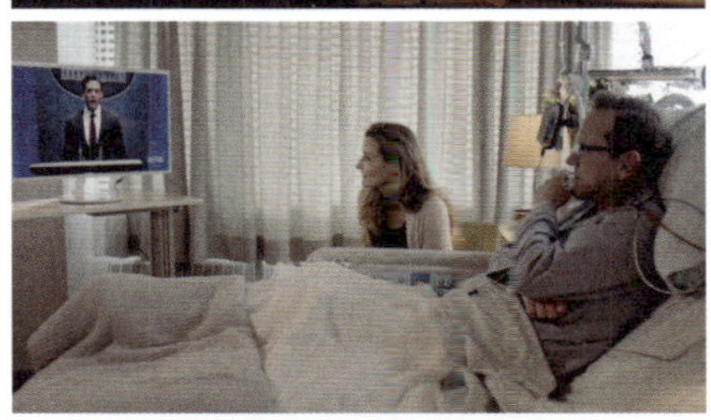

Pres. No.41

Pres.
No.44

Pres.
No.52

Pres.
No.54

Pres.
No.58

Pres.
No.59

Pres.
No.62

Pres.
No.63

Pres.
No.65

Pres.
No.66

Pres.
No.69

Pres.
No.72

Pres.
No.74

Pres.
No.77

Pres.
No.79

Pres.
No.82

Pres.
No.84

Pres.
No.86

Pres.
No.87

Pres.
No.89

Pres.
No.92

Pres.
No.95

Pres.
No.96

Pres.
No.98

Pres.
No.99

Pres.
No.102

Pres.
No.103

Pres.
No.104

Pres.
No.107

Pres.
No.108

Pres.
No.111

Pres.
No.112

Pres.
No.113

Pres.
No.114

Pres.
No.115

Pres.
No.119

Pres.
No.121

Pres.
No.122

Pres.
No.125

Pres.
No.127

Pres.
No.130

Pres.
No.131

Pres.
No.132

Pres.
No.139

Pres.
No.145

Pres.
No.147

Pres.
No.148

Pres.
No.153

Pres.
No.155

Pres.
No.157

Pres.
No.158

Pres.
No.161

Pres.
No.163

Pres.
No.164

Pres.
No.29

Pres.
No.93

Pres.
No.113

Pres.
No.137

Pres.
No.147

Pres.
No.148

Pres.
No.12

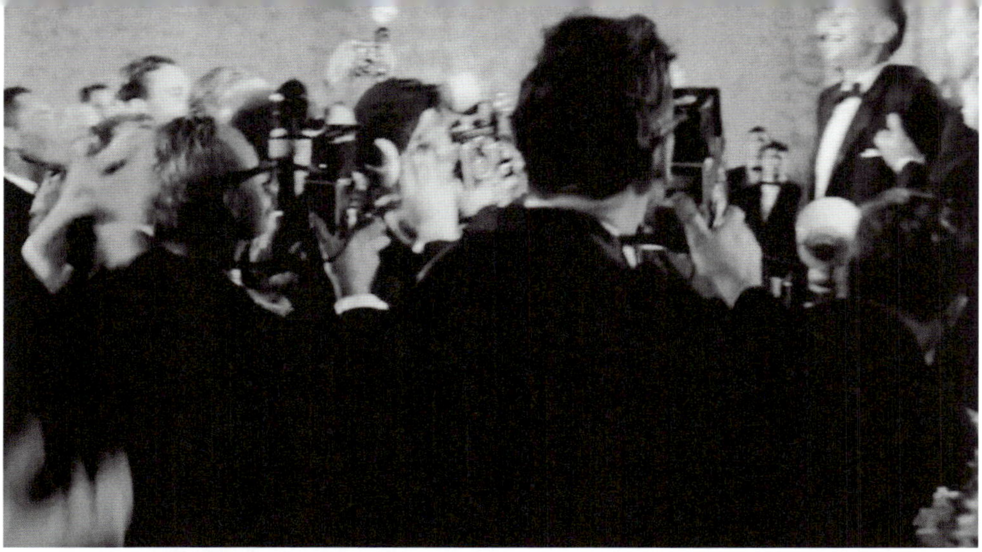

Pres.
No.95

Pres.
No.101

Pres. No.115

Pres. No.149

Pres. No.153

photographed by the press

Pres.
No.34

Pres.
No.91

Pres.
No.150

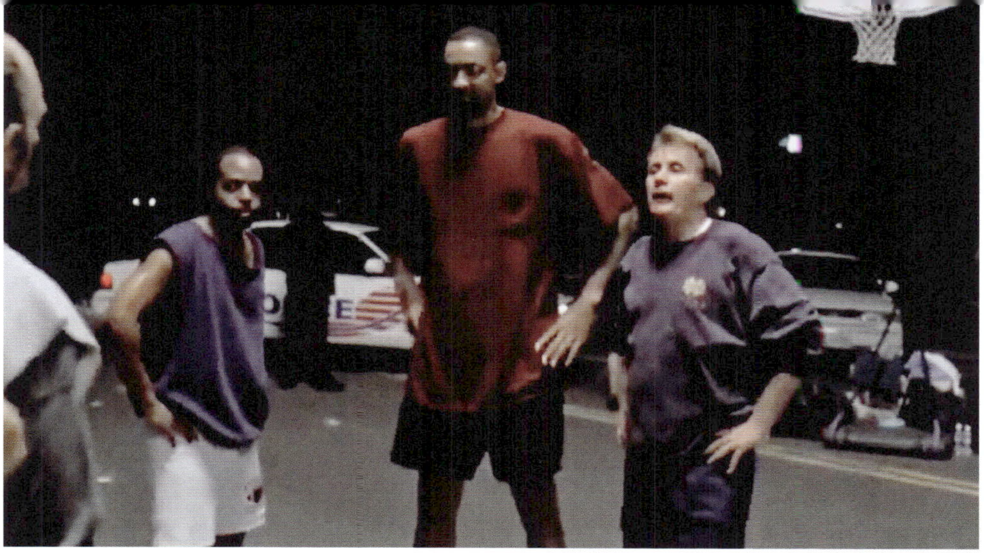

playing basketball

Pres.
No.92

playing golf

Pres.
No.95

Pres.
No.149

Pres.
No.157

Pres.
No.41

Pres.
No.132

Pres.
No.28

playing Scrabble

Pres.
No.39

praying

Pres.
No.130

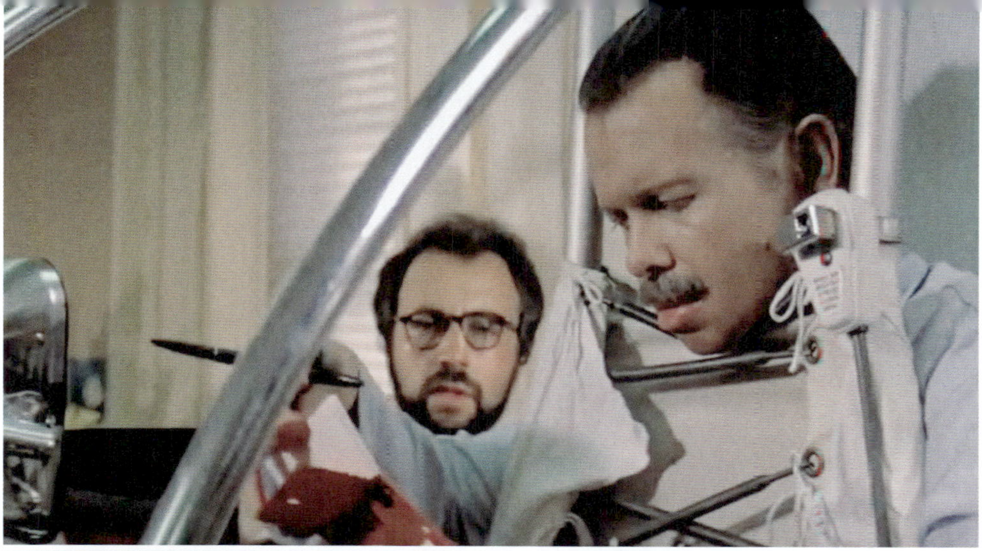

Pres.
No.132

Pres.
No.150

Pres.
No.2

Pres.
No.5

Pres.
No.14

Pres.
No.15

Pres.
No.16

Pres.
No.22

Pres.
No.24

Pres.
No.25

Pres.
No.30

Pres.
No.39

Pres.
No.46

Pres.
No.49

Pres.
No.50

Pres.
No.51

Pres.
No.56

Pres.
No.61

Pres.
No.65

Pres.
No.72

Pres.
No.75

Pres.
No.81

Pres.
No.86

Pres.
No.88

Pres.
No.89

Pres.
No.90

Pres.
No.92

Pres.
No.100

Pres.
No.102

Pres.
No.104

Pres.
No.108

Pres.
No.110

Pres.
No.111

Pres.
No.113

Pres.
No.116

Pres.
No.119

Pres.
No.124

Pres.
No.125

Pres.
No.126

Pres.
No.130

Pres.
No.132

Pres.
No.133

Pres.
No.135

Pres.
No.136

Pres.
No.140

Pres.
No.142

Pres.
No.144

Pres.
No.147

Pres.
No.150

Pres.
No.151

Pres.
No.153

Pres.
No.157

Pres.
No.160

Pres.
No.161

Pres.
No.162

Pres.
No.163

Pres.
No.164

Pres. No.18

Pres. No.23

Pres. No.25

Pres.
No.71

Pres.
No.92

Pres.
No.119

Pres.
No.150

Pres.
No.157

Pres.
No.16

relieved

Pres.
No.93

riding a horse

Pres.
No.68

Pres.
No.94

Pres.
No.34

riding a pig

Pres.
No.10

saluting

Pres.
No.15

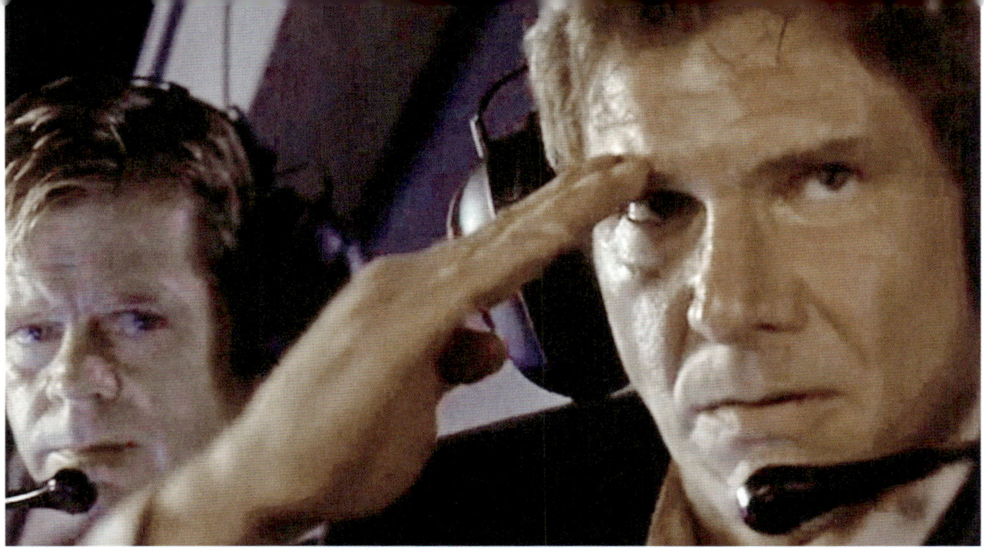

Pres.
No.71

Pres.
No.72

Pres.
No.74

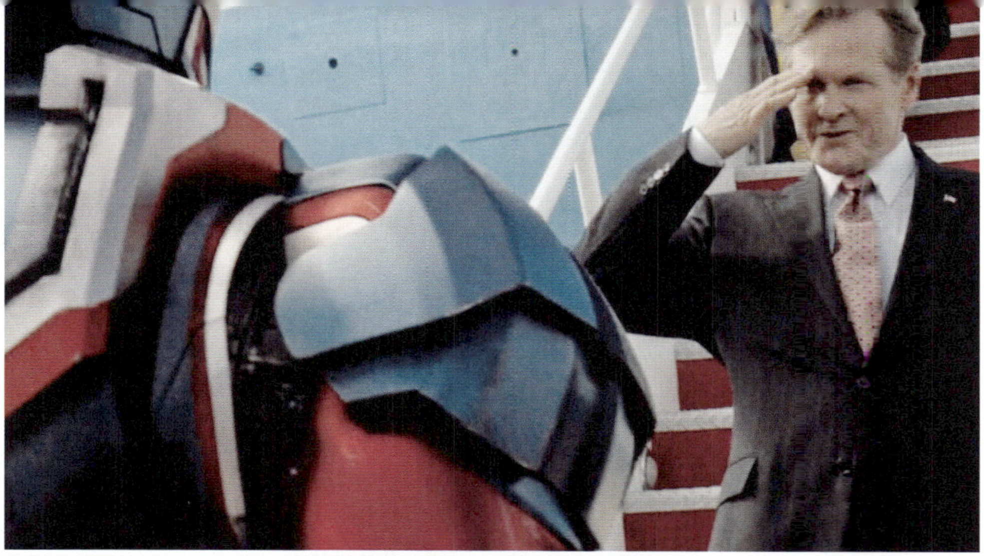

Pres.
No.94

Pres.
No.111

Pres.
No.118

Pres.
No.148

Pres.
No.158

Pres.
No.14

Pres.
No.25

Pres.
No.86

Pres.
No.116

Pres.
No.140

Pres.
No.1

Pres.
No.3

Pres.
No.13

Pres.
No.14

Pres.
No.16

Pres.
No.23

Pres.
No.25

Pres.
No.53

Pres.
No.57

Pres.
No.61

Pres.
No.71

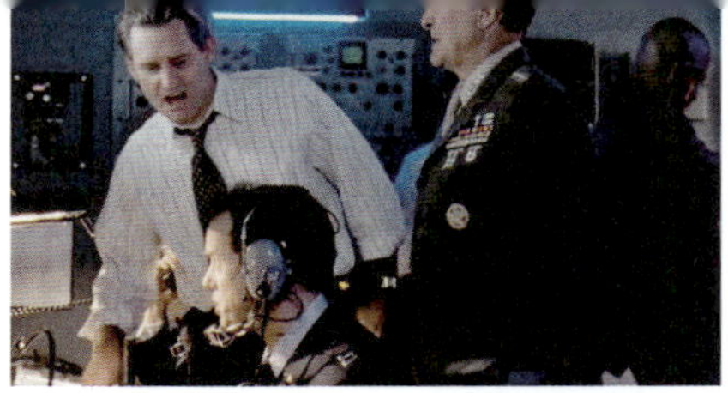

Pres.
No.86

Pres.
No.87

Pres.
No.98

Pres.
No.116

Pres.
No.132

Pres.
No.148

Pres.
No.149

Pres.
No.161

Pres.
No.163

Pres.
No.2

Pres.
No.5

Pres.
No.9

Pres.
No.12

Pres.
No.17

Pres.
No.18

Pres.
No.21

Pres.
No.22

Pres.
No.29

Pres.
No.32

Pres.
No.34

Pres.
No.41

Pres.
No.53

Pres.
No.54

Pres.
No.56

Pres.
No.58

Pres.
No.59

Pres.
No.65

Pres.
No.66

Pres.
No.70

Pres.
No.79

Pres.
No.84

Pres.
No.86

Pres.
No.87

Pres.
No.92

Pres.
No.101

Pres.
No.105

Pres.
No.109

Pres.
No.111

Pres.
No.129

Pres.
No.132

Pres.
No.137

Pres.
No.147

Pres.
No.148

Pres.
No.150

Pres.
No.151

Pres.
No.157

Pres.
No.158

Pres.
No.64

sharpening a pencil in his ear

Pres.
No.45

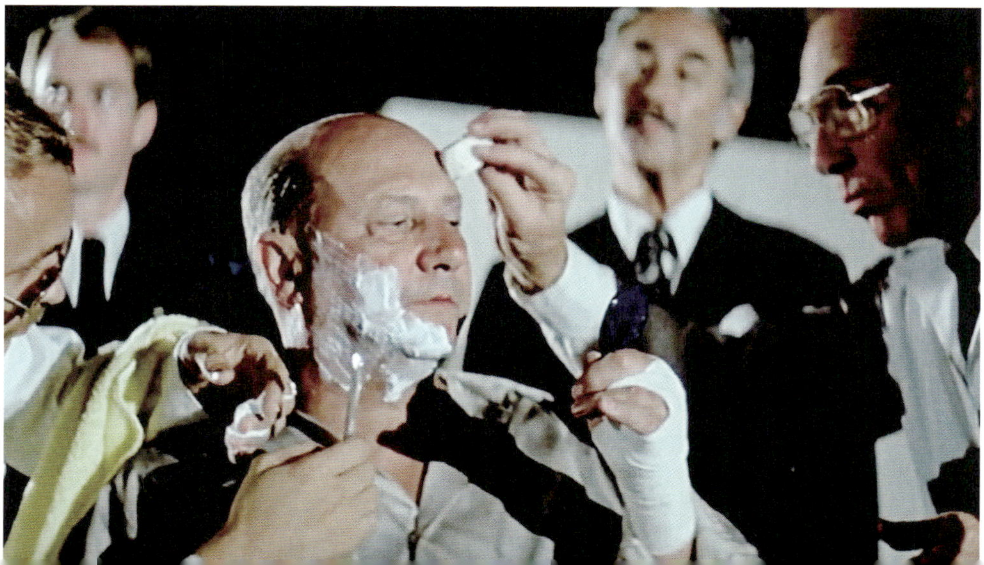

shaving

Pres.
No.151

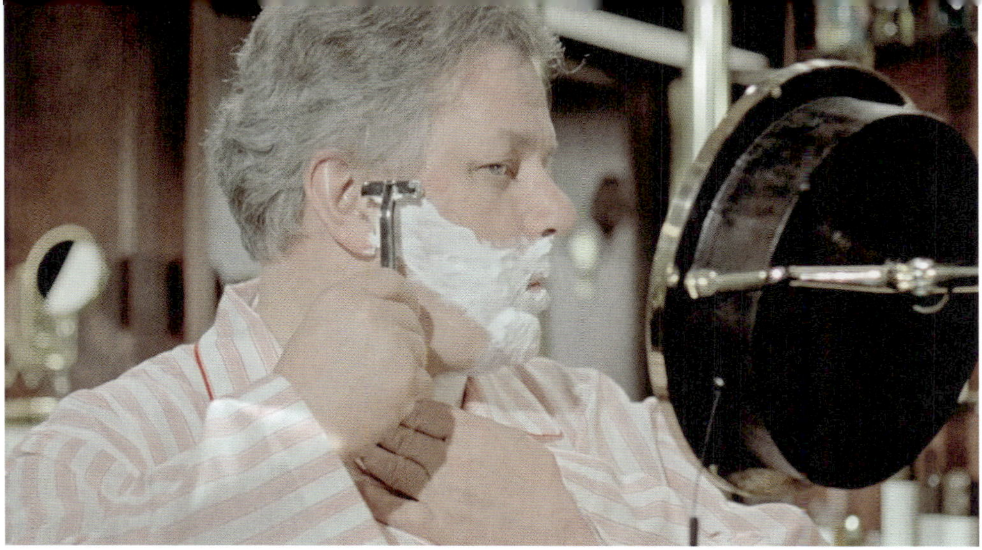

shaving

Pres.
No.16

shocked

Pres.
No.23

Pres.
No.25

Pres.
No.55

Pres.
No.59

Pres.
No.71

Pres.
No.101

Pres.
No.134

Pres.
No.151

Pres.
No.23

Pres.
No.45

Pres.
No.125

Pres.
No.158

shooting

Pres.
No.2

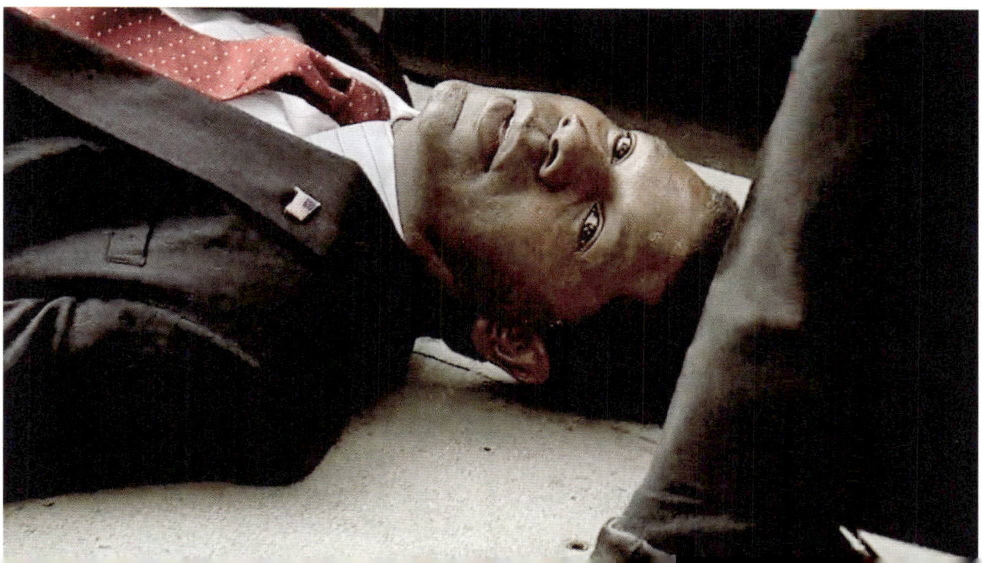

shot

Pres.
No.39

Pres.
No.54

Pres.
No.151

Pres.
No.153

Pres.
No.158

Pres.
No.33

sick in bed

Pres.
No.39

signing files

Pres.
No.47

Pres.
No.53

Pres.
No.56

Pres.
No.61

Pres.
No.64

Pres.
No.65

Pres.
No.83

Pres.
No.86

Pres.
No.112

Pres.
No.114

Pres.
No.115

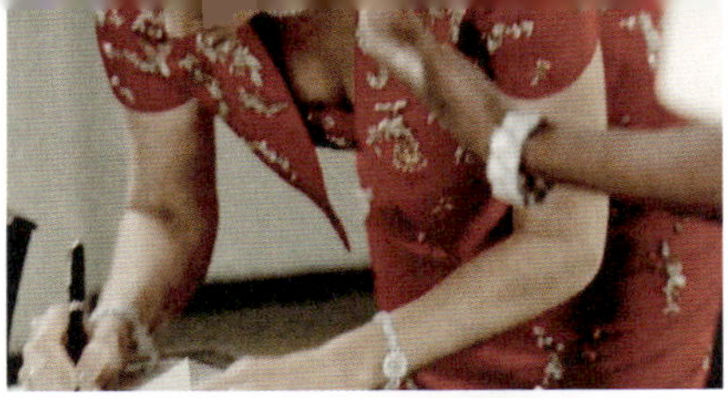

Pres.
No.135

Pres.
No.142

Pres.
No.147

Pres.
No.148

Pres.
No.66

Pres.
No.68

Pres.
No.84

Pres.
No.43

singing the national anthem

Pres.
No.1

sitting behind the desk addressing the nation

Pres.
No.19

Pres.
No.39

Pres.
No.86

Pres.
No.112

Pres.
No.118

Pres.
No.135

Pres.
No.161

Pres.
No.18

Pres.
No.29

Pres.
No.30

sitting on the desk in the Oval Office

Pres.
No.39

Pres.
No.58

Pres.
No.65

Pres.
No.79

Pres.
No.111

Pres.
No.125

Pres.
No.137

Pres.
No.40

sitting outside the Oval Office

Pres.
No.15

sleeping

Pres.
No.44

Pres.
No.47

Pres.
No.88

Pres.
No.100

Pres.
No.140

Pres.
No.149

Pres.
No.12

Pres.
No.41

Pres.
No.46

Pres.
No.58

Pres.
No.64

Pres.
No.66

Pres.
No.81

Pres.
No.119

Pres.
No.137

Pres.
No.39

Pres.
No.71

speaking to a crowd with a megaphone

Pres.
No.9

Pres.
No.160

Pres.
No.124

taking his shoes off

Pres.
No.9

talking to a boy

Pres.
No.17

Pres.
No.54

Pres.
No.92

Pres.
No.26

Pres.
No.41

Pres.
No.42

Pres.
No.44

Pres.
No.76

Pres.
No.160

Pres.
No.75

talking to her husband

Pres.
No.9

talking to his son

Pres.
No.98

talking to his son

Pres.
No.100

Pres.
No.28

Pres.
No.52

Pres.
No.66

Pres.
No.71

talking to his wife

Pres.
No.142

Pres.
No.147

Pres.
No.28

Pres.
No.30

Pres.
No.31

Pres. No.50

Pres. No.51

Pres. No.52

talking to their daughter

Pres.
No.2

Pres.
No.37

Pres.
No.59

Pres.
No.60

Pres.
No.61

Pres.
No.84

Pres.
No.131

Pres.
No.149

Pres.
No.39

Pres.
No.43

Pres.
No.51

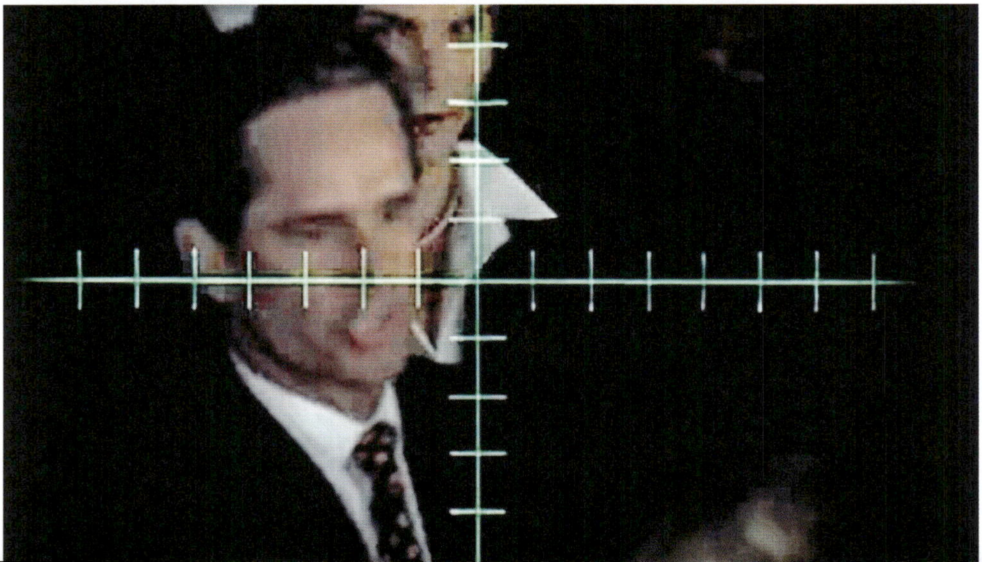

Pres.
No.104

Pres.
No.113

Pres.
No.115

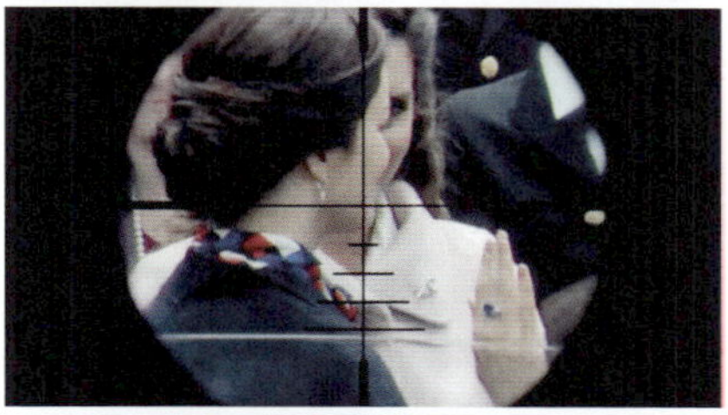

Pres.
No.121

Pres.
No.151

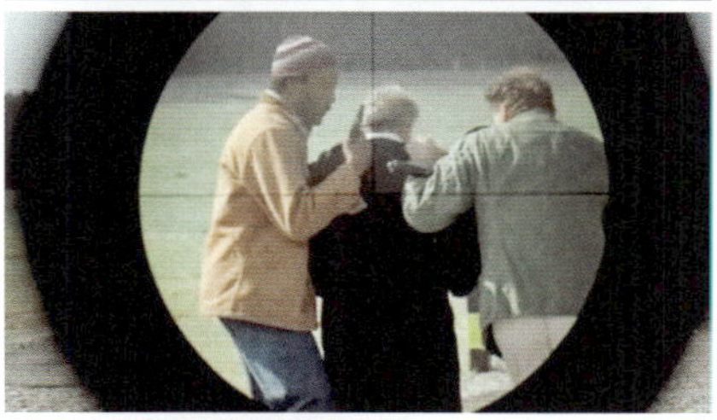

Pres.
No.153

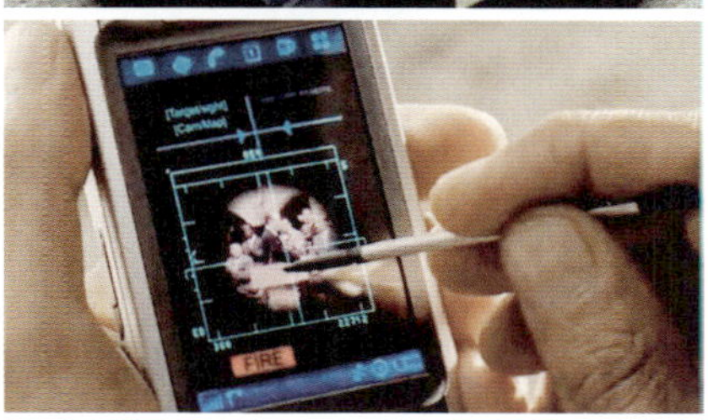

Pres.
No.30

Pres.
No.44

Pres.
No.74

Pres.
No.78

Pres.
No.119

Pres.
No.148

Pres.
No.15

Pres.
No.23

Pres.
No.26

Pres.
No.27

Pres.
No.39

Pres.
No.54

Pres.
No.57

Pres.
No.70

Pres.
No.76

Pres.
No.86

Pres.
No.87

Pres.
No.98

Pres.
No.101

Pres.
No.110

Pres.
No.112

Pres.
No.131

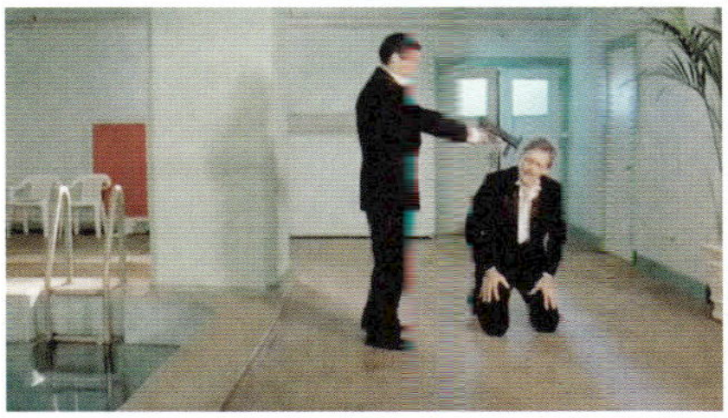

Pres.
No.142

Pres.
No.151

Pres.
No.153

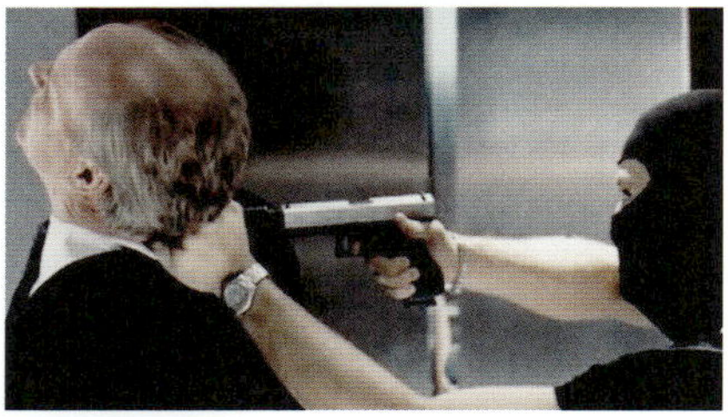

Pres.
No.158

Pres.
No.164

Pres.
No.14

typing in a code

Pres.
No.43

under fire

Pres.
No.52

Pres.
No.53

Pres.
No.57

Pres.
No.70

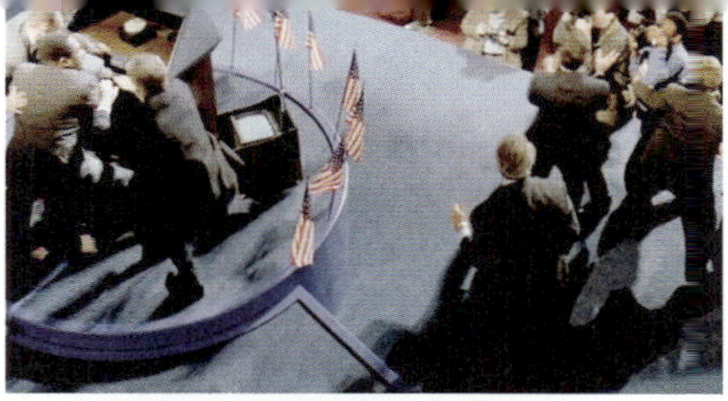

Pres.
No.79

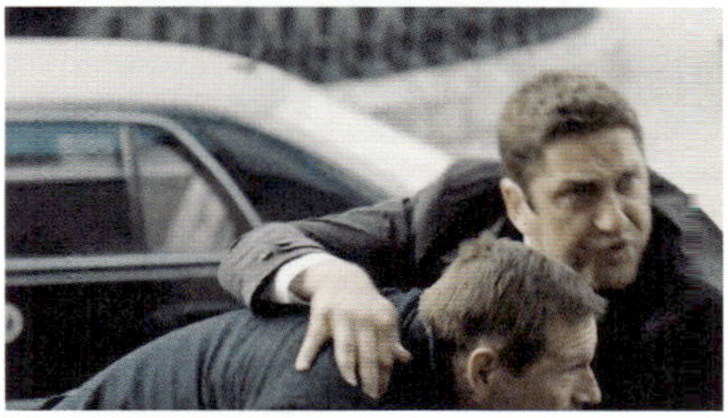

Pres.
No.110

Pres.
No.113

Pres.
No.121

Pres.
No.127

Pres.
No.128

Pres.
No.158

Pres.
No.64

vomiting

Pres.
No.48

waiting

Pres.
No.30

Pres.
No.132

Pres.
No.147

Pres.
No.64

washing dentures in the glass of another politician

Pres.
No.15

washing his face

Pres.
No.18

Pres.
No.19

Pres.
No.22

Pres.
No.29

Pres.
No.30

Pres.
No.39

Pres.
No.40

Pres.
No.59

Pres.
No.78

Pres.
No.86

Pres.
No.87

Pres.
No.95

Pres.
No.99

Pres.
No.124

Pres.
No.129

Pres.
No.130

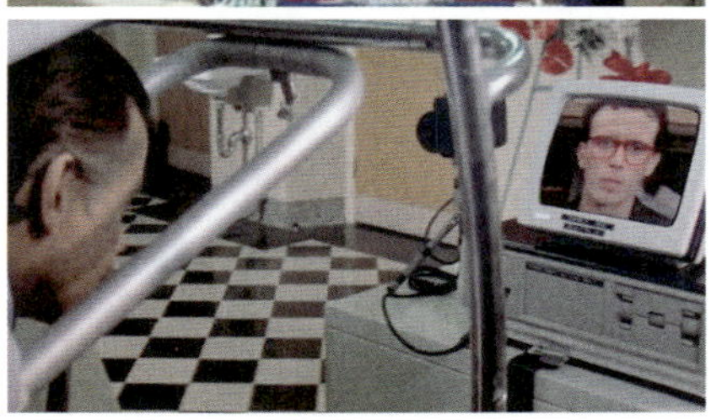

Pres.
No.138

Pres.
No.153

Pres.
No.156

Pres.
No.157

Pres.
No.161

Pres.
No.163

Pres.
No.2

Pres.
No.25

Pres.
No.28

Pres.
No.29

Pres.
No.33

Pres.
No.39

Pres.
No.58

Pres.
No.64

Pres.
No.65

Pres.
No.80

Pres.
No.81

Pres.
No.91

Pres.
No.101

Pres.
No.109

Pres.
No.115

Pres.
No.116

Pres.
No.131

Pres.
No.147

Pres.
No.148

Pres.
No.157

Pres.
No.164

Pres.
No.27

Pres.
No.141

Pres.
No.31

with a balloon animal

Pres.
No.116

with a bridal bouquet

Pres.
No.64

Pres.
No.124

Pres. No.34

Pres. No.49

Pres. No.59

Pres.
No.64

with a child

Pres.
No.79

with a crashed helicopter

Pres.
No.23

Pres.
No.25

Pres.
No.47

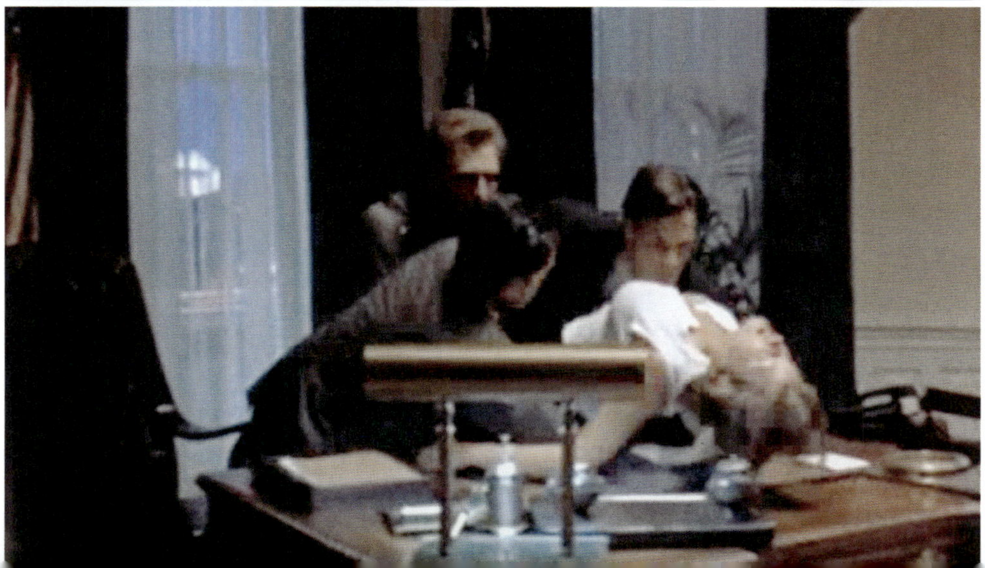

Pres.
No.71

with a dead body

Pres.
No.119

with a doctor

Pres.
No.150

with a doctor

Pres.
No.28

with a dog

Pres.
No.29

Pres.
No.33

Pres.
No.34

Pres. No.157

Pres. No.161

Pres.
No.15

Pres.
No.23

Pres.
No.26

Pres.
No.49

Pres.
No.53

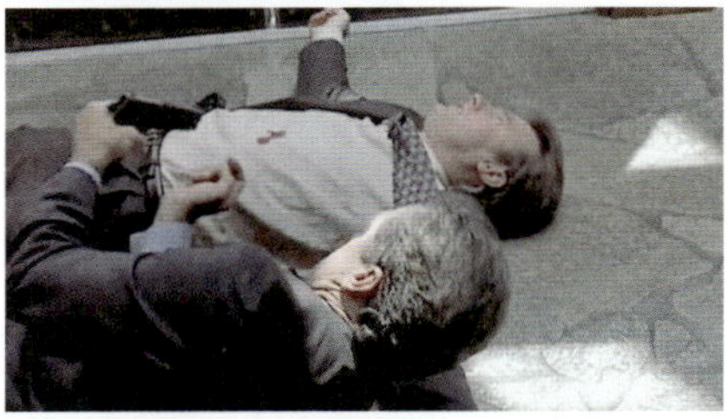

Pres.
No.54

Pres.
No.68

Pres.
No.76

Pres.
No.81

Pres.
No.82

Pres.
No.87

Pres.
No.98

Pres.
No.120

Pres.
No.125

Pres.
No.158

Pres.
No.54

Pres.
No.58

Pres.
No.49

Pres.
No.54

Pres.
No.71

Pres.
No.86

Pres.
No.116

Pres.
No.163

Pres.
No.23

with a signal flare

Pres.
No.26

with a superhero

Pres.
No.36

Pres.
No.74

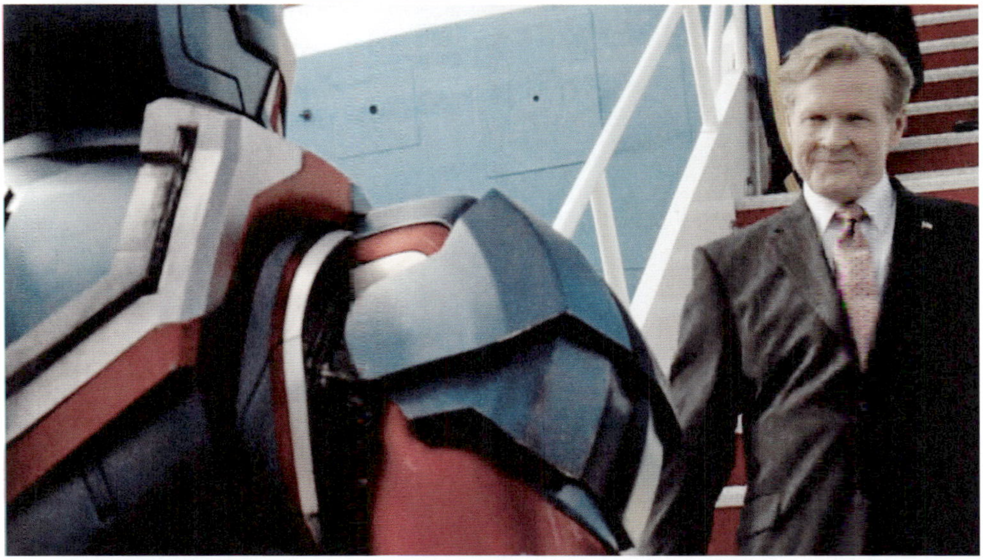

Pres.
No.128

Pres.
No.2

with confidential files

Pres.
No.64

with dentures

Pres.
No.26

Pres.
No.55

Pres.
No.137

Pres.
No.15

with his daughter

Pres.
No.28

Pres.
No.50

Pres.
No.52

Pres.
No.71

Pres.
No.141

with his daughter

Pres.
No.33

Pres.
No.34

Pres.
No.54

Pres. No.52

Pres. No.69

Pres. No.71

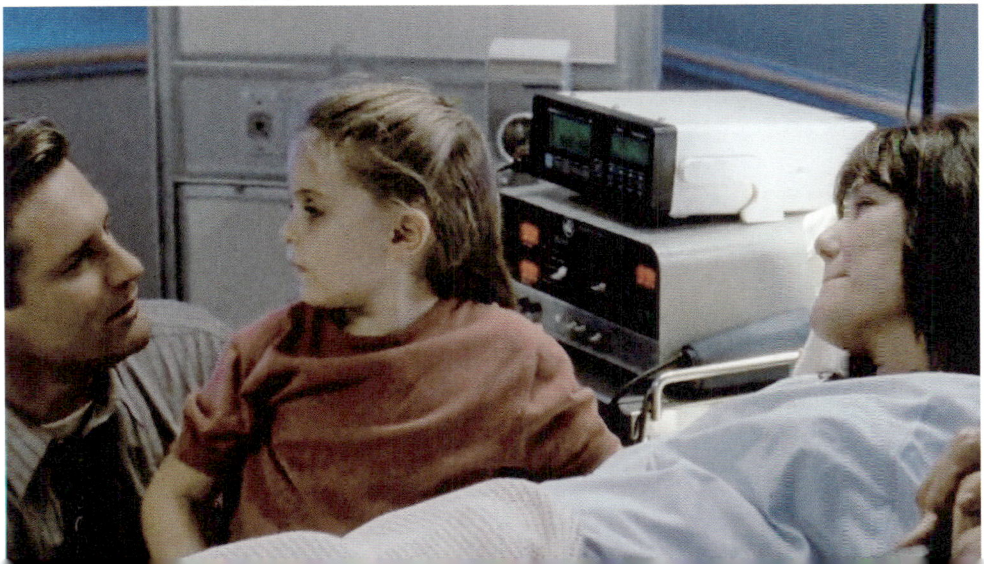

with his family

Pres.
No.141

with his family

Pres.
No.113

with his mistress

Pres.
No.1

Pres.
No.8

Pres.
No.14

Pres.
No.15

Pres.
No.28

Pres.
No.39

Pres.
No.50

Pres.
No.64

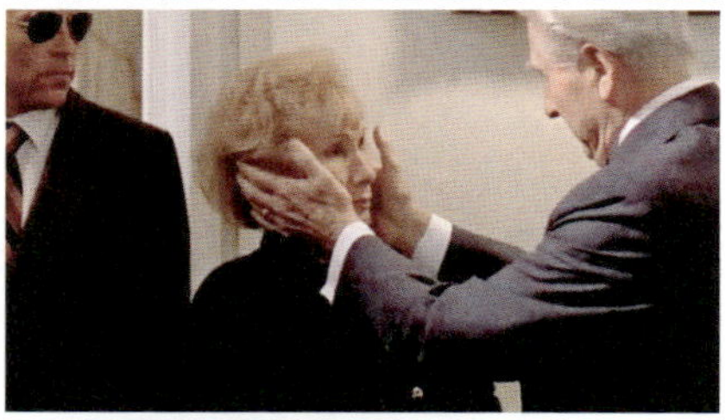

Pres.
No.66

Pres.
No.92

Pres.
No.98

Pres.
No.113

Pres.
No.131

Pres.
No.135

Pres.
No.141

Pres.
No.34

with robot arms

Pres.
No.44

with the military

Pres.
No.73

with the military

Pres.
No.41

with the nuclear briefcase

Pres.
No.54

Pres.
No.110

Pres.
No.111

Pres.
No.112

Pres.
No.161

Pres.
No.24

Pres.
No.110

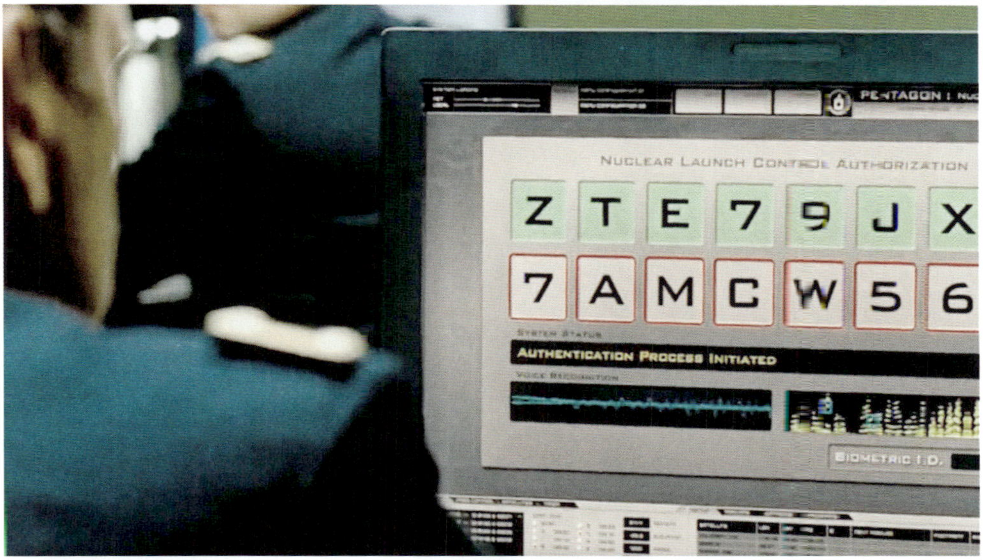

Pres.
No.111

Pres.
No.112

Pres.
No.148

Pres.
No.3

Pres.
No.39

Pres.
No.48

with the officer who is carrying the nuclear briefcase

Pres.
No.71

Pres.
No.83

Pres.
No.99

Pres.
No.112

Pres.
No.148

Pres.
No.161

with the officer who is carrying the nuclear briefcase

Pres.
No.2

Pres.
No.8

Pres.
No.13

Pres.
No.28

Pres.
No.32

Pres.
No.34

Pres.
No.37

Pres.
No.39

Pres.
No.60

Pres.
No.110

Pres.
No.116

Pres.
No.161

Pres.
No.66

Pres.
No.83

Pres.
No.86

Pres.
No.96

Pres.
No.104

Pres.
No.114

Pres.
No.129

Pres.
No.132

Pres.
No.18

working in bed

Pres.
No.30

working late

Pres.
No.49

Pres.
No.56

Pres.
No.104

Pres.
No.124

working late

Pres.
No.39

working on a computer

Pres.
No.58

Pres.
No.66

Pres.
No.115

Pres.
No.22

Pres.
No.58

Pres.
No.79

Pres.
No.95

Pres.
No.157

Pres.
No.161

Pres.
No.23

wrapped in a blanket

Pres.
No.15

writing

United Presidents of America
[Essay by Teresa Rudolf]

PRESIDENTIAL CHRONOLOGY

Hardly any other figure in the modern era has been depicted in so many different ways as the President of the United States of America. Often referred to as "the most powerful man in the world," representations of this figure not only reflect the national historical narrative but also offer a genealogy of how the president has been imagined over time.

George Washington, elected the first president of the United States in 1789, has been followed by forty-four incumbents. As a fixed part of the president's official title, this consecutive numbering offers a rather distinctive way of measuring the age of American democracy. The naming process itself suggests a classical antagonism: the numbering refers to the person and not the term of office, for example, and this alludes to the ongoing continuity of the presidency as well as the exchangeability of the person occupying it. This opens up a fundamental conflict in the mode of representation whose origins go back much further than the founding of the United States of America: the conflict between the office and the natural person.

THE PRESIDENT'S "TWO BODIES"

Rulers have always sought to cultivate their political image. In the modern era, the tradition of portraying rulers reached its zenith with the Baroque style of distinguished painting, which introduced an entire system of production (including court painters) and institutionalized conventions of representation. Whereas the bourgeoisie, for example, were only permitted to have themselves depicted in *private* half-length portraits, the full-length portrait was reserved for the sovereign. While the exercise of power in the Early and High Middle Ages depended upon the king's personal presence, as God's representative he eludes figurative depiction in Baroque painting. As not even the laws of geometric perspective could be allowed to stand above the sovereign, his aloofness was often reinforced by the addition of nebulous *sfumato*. Whereas these prestigious forms of representation were regulated by strict codes, today there are more complex and nuanced means of producing, publishing, and distributing images of rulers. Here, Donald Trump's Twitter entries, Barack Obama's Instagram posts, and Angela Merkel's televised addresses offer completely different examples of how political iconography can be disseminated today.

In 1957 the historian Ernst Kantorowicz, who had emigrated from Nazi Germany to Princeton in the United States, published his seminal book *The King's Two Bodies*, in which he presented the concept of "dynastic continuity": "The perpetuity of the head of the realm and the concept of a *rex qui nunquam moritur*, a 'king that never dies,' depended mainly on the interplay of three factors: the perpetuity of the Dynasty, the corporate character of the Crown, and the immortality of the royal Dignity."[1] Thus, the ruler always had more than just one body: the immortal political body ("body politic") of the king, with which he commanded the monarchy by virtue of his power and dignity, is thus different from his mortal, biological body ("body natural"). This binary understanding of the body—of the private person versus the statesman or stateswoman—can also be applied to representations of modern political systems.

In line with this symbolic notion of the body, staged rituals have been used to define political life ever since the premodern era. Heraldic devices, emblems, flags, and written and painted portraits have represented the political order in symbolic terms. Should the person die, the office lives on—*Le roi est mort, vive le roi!*[2] It is a paradox that the ruler's power becomes most visible in absentia, when he or she dies.

In popular culture, we see how stately self-staging culminates in exaggerated stereotypical representations of power. In film, such representations are often expressed in the form of historical figures. However, the unique nature of the American president has led to the development of an entire genre of cinematic fiction in which the iconography of political reality is reproduced and augmented.

• addressing Congress [p. 48]
• briefing staff [p. 95]

In film, the body politic of the head of state and military commander in chief is portrayed primarily in

• giving a speech [p. 150]
• in a meeting [p. 202]
• in a meeting with the military [p. 214]
• in a meeting in the Oval Office [p. 208]
• with confidential files [p. 406]

the form of public sessions, briefings, and confidential discussions with staff. The figure at the center of these meetings is often identified solely by a small version of the Stars and Stripes pinned to his or her lapel. In the real world, Barack Obama could often be seen wearing just such a pin, too.

In recent times, the effective public use of clothing as a conveyor of meaning can be seen, for example, in how Donald Trump has projected himself since the beginning of his candidacy. Harkening back to a circular pin from Ronald Reagan's campaign in the early 1980s,[3] Reagan's slogan of "Let's Make America Great Again" was reborn on Trump's bright-red baseball cap as "Make America Great Again." Invariably appearing in his idiosyncratic dark-blue suit, white shirt, and red tie, and posing with a thumbs-up gesture, the entrepreneur and billionaire Trump has styled himself the living embodiment of the U.S. flag and the messiah of an American "self-made" affirmation of the future.

Pres. No. 89 • getting out of the car [p. 144]
• looking at a painting [p. 259]

Whereas male presidents in film are easily identified by their typically dark suits, female heads of state have more room for extravagance, as we can see in the leopard-print pumps worn by former British prime minister Theresa May. This expanded dress code symbolizes the role of women in the political sphere, which is in a process of redefinition. Notably, the monochrome pantsuits worn by German chancellor Angela Merkel often serve as projection screens, and, as a supposed mood barometer, they are used to try to take a reading on the current political situation.

Pres. No. 117 • in a school class [p. 218]
Pres. No. 64 • with a child [p. 393]
• as a hostage [p. 57]
• kissing [p. 250]
• killing [p. 250]
• with a dog [p. 396]
• with a gun [p. 399]

This kind of self-staging as a means to generate an identity is a fundamental part of creating an *image* that is maintained and reproduced in the media. For example, during his public appearances, Adolf Hitler's personal photographer Heinrich Hoffmann often placed him in direct contact with children in order to promote the image of an empathic and approachable head of state. In accordance with the generation of this public image, the leader often embodies "good" and "evil" to equal degrees—after all, his or her duty to protect the nation and the state can lead to his limiting the freedoms of his subjects. Whereas the conflict with political foes takes on abstract forms in institutional decision-making processes (the term "Axis of Evil" coined by George W. Bush offers a metaphor for this), fictive American presidents in film often take part personally in the fight against evil or even appear as kidnapping victims (*Behind Enemy Lines II: Axis of Evil, 2006*).

- bloodied [p. 88]
- fighting [p. 123]
- in a video conference with a terrorist [p. 223]
- shooting [p. 338]
- with a gun [p. 399]

Pres. No. 21

In keeping with the tradition in politics and political references afforded by slogans and symbols, we can also make out a distinctive genealogy of fictional presidents running through cinematic history. Antagonism between the public person and the natural person spins a web of diegetic and intertextual complexity. In the film *Scary Movie, 2003*, an imaginary president looks at the framed portrait of another fictive president from the film *Air Force One, 1997*, which hangs on the wall as a kind of legitimization of this invented presidential family tree. Such references can be generated at the level of movie roles or actor filmographies.

Pres. No. 116
- looking at a painting [p. 259]

Pres. No. 15

In instances where a film seeks to highlight a private moment in a president's everyday working life, this (usually male) head of state is shown enjoying a glass of hard liquor. Remarkably often, the "father of the nation" is depicted as the father of a daughter in his private life. In the film *First Daughter, 2004*, the president's teenage daughter's life stands as a metaphor for the need for family privacy. In the real political world, the political achievements of presidents such as John F. Kennedy and Bill Clinton are forced into the background, not least because of the anecdotes pertaining to their private love lives.

- bowling [p. 95]
- drinking alcohol [p. 113]
- playing pool [p. 309]
- smoking [p. 354]

Pres. No. 50
- eating cake [p. 120]
- talking to his daughter [p. 367]
- with his daughter [p. 408]

THE ARCHITECTURE OF POWER

The spatial manifestation of American power is the Oval Office in the White House. The room's elliptical shape gives rise to a particular constellation during group meetings in terms of seating and eye contact: the president's position at the head of the room enables him to maintain eye contact with everyone and gives him an overview of all of the participants. In scenes both fictional and real, these key arenas of political ac-

- behind the desk in the Oval Office [p. 71]
- in the Oval Office talking to the staff [p. 95]
- looking out the window of the Oval Office [p. 113]
- in a meeting at the Oval Office [p. 208]
- sitting on the desk in the Oval Office [p. 309]

tion are framed by prestigious architecture, which usually consists of sacred elements. Here, features such as flags serve as symbols of a state framework generating a sense of identity.

• campaigning [p. 103]
• giving a press conference [p. 146]

Global power relationships find their embodiment in a single item in the White House dating from the Cold War: the "red telephone" offering direct communication between Washington and Moscow has served as an instrument of de-escalation in crisis situations ever since it was introduced in 1963. Stanley Kubrick's 1964 film *Dr. Strangelove* or: *How I Learned to Stop Worrying and Love the Bomb* can be interpreted as a direct cinematic response to this novelty in the history of diplomacy and communications technology. Even today, and with remarkable frequency, presidents in films tend to be shown speaking into analog landline devices instead of mobile phones, for example.

• on the red telephone [p. 288]
Pres. No. 42
• on the cell phone [p. 284]
• on the telephone [p. 289]

By contrast, the symmetrical, concentric arrangement of the Speaker's podium in the U.S. House of Representatives is, as in older parliaments, reminiscent of the sacral architecture of a church choir. Whereas its bombastic exaggeration often gives it the appearance of a film set, at least to European eyes, increased security measures in place since the turn of the millennium have often required U.S. presidents to hold their public speeches from behind a head-high structure of bulletproof glass. If one examines footage of such presidential appearances, it is possible to make out an analogous, nearly identical composition: usually the president is shown from behind facing a mass of onlookers. In these visually staged addresses, the crowd always represents the "body" of the people symbolizing the power rooted within it. Looking from the other perspective, namely the president's view of the popular "body," his role as a democratic representative is made manifest. Here one might remember Thomas Hobbes's *Leviathan*, whose frontispiece by Abraham Bosse, drawn in 1651, depicts a ruler composed of countless human bodies. Only the head appears to rise above the mass of people as a "surplus."

• addressing Congress [p. 48]
• at the inauguration [p. 67]
• giving a speech [p. 150]
Pres. No. 39 • at the inauguration [p. 67]
Pres. No. 57 • campaigning [p. 103]
Pres. No. 104 • campaigning [p. 104]

• in the Situation Room [p. 244]

Of the White House's three highly secure conference rooms, the most important is the Situation Room, a communications center that has found a place in our collective visual memory, especially since the appearance of a press photo dated May 1, 2011, that shows Barack Obama surrounded by his key officials during the military operation against Osama bin Laden. As the U.S. government decided not to publish images of Bin Laden's corpse, in accordance with international ethical standards, the Situation Room photograph became a visual symbol of Operation Neptune Spear. Pete Souza, the Chief Official White House Photographer, was the only photographer to capture an image of this seminal meeting. In abstract terms, the photo symbolizes a historical event that is taking place outside of the depicted space. We see a group of figures made up of representatives of the government and military. Only Hillary Clinton's emotional gesture as she holds her hand in front of her mouth offers any indication of the situation's exceptional importance. As parts of the image were blurred and the figures in the photograph could not be identified clearly, the photo soon became, for this and other reasons, the object of intense public discussion and an occasion for conspiracy theories. The photo, which symbolizes the asymmetrical warfare being waged against terrorism, has been invoked in *House of Cards* by showing a similar arrangement of figures.

Pres. No.67 • in the Situation Room [p. 246]

According to the visual historian Horst Bredekamp, it is possible to differentiate between "images of memory" and "images inspiring action."[5] These two notions are representative of the discussions surrounding the institutionalized production of images and strategic visual politics. Whereas the democratic understanding of the journalistic system sees it as a means of public control, a competing system arose in the United States in the 1960s with the arrival of highly professional public relations campaigns conducted by the U.S. government. The White House's production of its own photographs distributed to journalists generates conflicting priorities of image curation and censorship.

John F. Kennedy was the first president to hire an official presidential photographer, Cecil W. Stoughton, for the White House in 1961. During the short thirty-four months of Kennedy's presidency before he was murdered in 1963, Stoughton produced around 12,000 photographs of the president.[6] After Kennedy's death, critical photographs that could have damaged the deceased statesman's reputation were removed from this collection. It is for this reason that only a single photograph showing the president together with his alleged lover, the actress Marilyn Monroe, has survived this posthumous historiographical cleansing.

Pres. No.19 • in bed with his mistress [p. 229]
Pres. No.11 • kissing his mistress [p. 253]
Pres. No.113 • kissing his mistress [p. 253]
• with his mistress [p. 412]

Hardly any other photograph has captured the close kinship between the presidency and show business so concisely as the portrait of Ronald Reagan taken by presidential photographer Michael Evans showing the president wearing a cowboy hat. Having been hospitalized after receiving a gunshot wound during an assassination attempt in 1985, Reagan was persistently pictured convalescing, and he too became an example of modern-day image censorship: all of the intravenous tubes were removed from photographs of the president. Even President Roosevelt banned the publication of any photographs depicting him in a wheelchair at an advanced age. Just like in classical portraits of leaders, in modern times, too, weakness is not compatible with the image of a head of state.

• in the hospital [p. 234]
• injured [p. 248]

As President Obama had over 6,668 images of his daily political dealings and private life published on social media—first and foremost the photo platform Flickr—his presidency soon came to be known as the "Flickr presidency."[7] It was something of a sensation when, at the funeral service for Nelson Mandela, Obama took a selfie of himself together with British prime minister David Cameron and Danish prime minister Helle Thorning-Schmidt. As the art historian Wolfgang Ullrich noted, it was not the selfie itself that caused a stir but the photograph of this bizarre scene taken by a journalist, which led to intense discussion in the press.[8]

THE FUTURE PRESIDENT

There is a prophetic dimension to the satirical exaggeration and fantasy presented in films. An episode of the American cartoon series *The Simpsons* from 2000 but set in the year 2030 anticipated the presidency of the entrepreneur and playboy Donald Trump. Similarly, other films have anticipated the historical arrival of female, black, and Latino U.S. presidents.

As politics also functions via the creation of images, this reciprocal relationship between fact and fiction can be re-enacted in daily political life. If the actual president at any given time is characterized by a comprehensive culture of presidential representation, this image is reproduced by means of a complex political apparatus that the public has come to expect. In a world dominated by imagery, fictions are likewise capable of redefining and shaping our image of the "Most Powerful Man in the World."

1 Ernst Kantorowicz, *The King's Two Bodies: A Study in Medieval Political Theology*, Princeton: Princeton University Press, 1997, p. 316.
2 See Ulrich Pfisterer, "Zwei Körper des Königs," in *Politische Ikonographie: Ein Handbuch*, vol. 2, Imperator bis Zwerg, ed. Uwe Fleckner, Martin Warnke, and Hendrik Ziegler, Munich: C.H. Beck, 2014, p. 559.
3 Ronald Reagan (1911–2004) was the 40th President of the United States of America from 1981 to 1989.
4 George W. Bush (born 1946) was the 43rd President of the United States of America from 2001 to 2009.
5 Horst Bredekamp, "Souverän ist, wer mit den Bildern entscheidet," in *Staatserzählungen: Die Deutschen und ihre politische Ordnung*, ed. Herfried Münkler et. al., Berlin: Rowohlt Verlag, 2018, pp. 127–142.
6 www.nytimes.com/2008/11/06/arts/design/06stoughton.html (last accessed on February 1, 2020)
7 www.flickr.com/people/obamawhitehouse/ (last accessed on February 1, 2020)
8 See Wolfgang Ulrich, *Selfies*, Berlin: Wagenbach Klaus GmbH, 2019.

Index Presidents 1–164

[Presidents, Movies/Series, Years, Actors, and Illustration Index]

Pres.
No.1

PRESIDENT
PAUL HOGLLISTER
"10.5: Apocalypse"
2006
Played by
Beau Bridges

- addressing the nation on TV [p.51]
- behind the desk in the Oval Office [p.71]
- broadcast on TV [p.99]
- crying [p.105]
- drinking coffee [p.111]
- frustrated [p.129]
- helpless [p.169]
- his wife holding his face [p.173]
- hugging his wife [p.175]
- in a meeting [p.202]
- on the telephone [p.289]
- on the telephone, looking at files [p.295]
- screaming [p.327]
- sitting on the desk in the Oval Office addressing the nation [p.346]
- with his wife [p.413]

Produced by
- Hallmark Entertainment
- Pear Pictures
- Jaffe/Braunstein Films
- Muse Entertain-ment Enterprises

Pres.
No.2

PRESIDENT
DAVID PALMER
"24"
2002–2004
Played by
Dennis Haysbert

- behind his desk in the Oval Office, talking to the staff [p.76]
- being briefed [p.81]
- greeting a crowd [p.158]
- in a meeting [p.203]
- in a meeting room [p.212]
- in a video conference [p.220]
- on the telephone [p.289]
- on TV [p.296]
- reading files [p.312]
- shaking hands [p.330]
- shot [p.339]
- talking to the press [p.368]
- waving [p.386]
- with confidential files [p.406]
- with the Secret Service [p.423]

Produced by
- Imagine Television
- Real Time Productions
- Teakwood Lane Productions
- 20th Century Fox Television

Pres.
No.3

PRESIDENT
JOHN KEELER
"24"
2005
Played by
Geoffrey Pierson

- addressing the nation on TV [p.51]
- in a conversation [p.190]
- in a meeting [p.203]
- in a video conference [p.221]
- in the office on board Air Force One [p.239]
- on the telephone [p.289]
- screaming [p.327]
- with the officer who is carrying the nuclear briefcase [p.421]

Produced by
- Imagine Television
- Real Time Productions
- Teakwood Lane Productions
- 20th Century Fox Television

Pres.
No.4

PRESIDENT
CHARLES LOGAN
"24"
2005–2007
Played by
Gregory Itzin

- briefing staff [p.95]
- broadcast on TV [p.99]
- giving a speech [p.150]
- hugging his wife [p.175]
- in a video conference [p.221]

Produced by
- Imagine Television
- Real Time Productions
- Teakwood Lane Productions
- 20th Century Fox Television

Pres.
No.5

PRESIDENT
WAYNE PALMER
"24"
2007
Played by
D. B. Woodside

- addressing the nation on TV [p.51]
- behind the desk in the Oval Office [p.71]
- behind his desk in the Oval Office, talking to the staff [p.76]
- being briefed [p.81]
- broadcast on TV [p.99]
- giving a press conference [p.146]
- helpless [p.169]
- in a crisis situation [p.196]
- in a meeting with the military [p.214]
- in the Oval Office talking to the staff [p.241]
- looking shocked at a screen [p.270]
- reading files [p.312]
- shaking hands [p.330]

Produced by
- Imagine Television
- Real Time Productions
- Teakwood Lane Productions
- 20th Century Fox Television

Pres.
No.6

PRESIDENT
NOAH DANIELS
"24"
2007
Played by
Powers Boothe

- in a meeting [p.203]
- in a meeting room [p.212]
- in the Situation Room [p.244]
- looking at a screen [p.260]

Produced by
- Imagine Television
- Real Time Productions
- Teakwood Lane Productions
- 20th Century Fox Television

Pres.
No.7

PRESIDENT
ALLISON TAYLOR
"24"
2009
Played by
Cherry Jones

- behind her desk in the Oval Office, talking to the staff [p.76]
- in a meeting [p.204]
- looking out the window of the Oval Office [p.268]
- on the telephone [p.290]
- on the telephone, looking at files [p.295]

Produced by
- Imagine Television
- Real Time Productions
- Teakwood Lane Productions
- 20th Century Fox Television

Pres.
No.8

PRESIDENT
JAMES HELLER
"24"
2010
Played by
William Devane

- drinking coffee [p.111]
- in a car [p.183]
- in a conversation [p.190]
- with his wife [p.413]
- with the Secret Service [p.423]

Produced by
- Imagine Television
- Real Time Productions
- Teakwood Lane Productions
- 20th Century Fox Television

Pres.
No.9

PRESIDENT
DALE GILCHRIST
"1600 Penn"
2012–2013
Played by
Bill Pullman

- at a banquet [p.60]
- drinking alcohol [p.113]
- fighting [p.123]
- fishing [p.125]
- getting dressed [p.132]
- giving an interview with his wife [p.146]
- giving a press conference [p.146]
- having breakfast [p.164]
- having dinner [p.167]
- hugging his daughter [p.177]
- in a conversation [p.190]
- in a meeting [p.204]
- in a meeting with the military [p.214]
- in bed [p.226]
- in bed with his wife [p.230]
- kissing [p.250]
- looking out the window of the Oval Office [p.268]
- on TV [p.296]
- shaking hands [p.330]
- swimming [p.357]
- talking to a boy [p.358]
- talking to his son [p.362]

Produced by
- Angry Child Productions
- Small Dog Picture Company
- 20th Century Fox Television
- Cinema Vehicle Services

Pres.
No.10

PRESIDENT
THOMAS WILSON
"2012"
2009
Played by
Danny Glover

- addressing the nation on TV [p.52]
- behind the desk in the Oval Office [p.71]
- briefing staff [p.96]

- broadcast on TV [p.100]
- in a church [p.187]
- in a video conference [p.221]
- meeting another politician [p.272]
- on the cell phone [p.284]
- saluting [p.321]

Produced by
- Columbia Pictures
- Centropolis Entertainment
- Farewell Productions
- The Mark Gordon Company

Pres. No.11

PRESIDENT
ALAN RICHMOND
“Absolute Power”
1997
Played by
Gene Hackman

- abusing a woman [p.48]
- addressing the nation on TV [p.52]
- behind his desk in the Oval Office, talking to the staff [p.77]
- dead [p.108]
- giving a press conference [p.146]
- giving a speech [p.150]
- killing [p.250]
- kissing his mistress [p.253]
- looking out the window of the Oval Office [p.268]
- on TV [p.296]

Produced by
- Columbia Pictures
- Castle Rock Entertainment
- Malpaso Productions

Pres. No.12

THE PRESIDENT OF THE UNITED STATES OF AMERICA
“Advise and Consent”
1962
Played by
Franchot Tone

- behind the desk in the Oval Office [p.72]
- behind his desk in the Oval Office, talking to the staff [p.77]
- giving a speech [p.150]
- in a bathrobe [p.179]
- in a conversation [p.191]
- in the Oval Office talking to the staff [p.241]
- looking out the window of the Oval Office [p.269]
- on the telephone [p.290]
- photographed by the press [p.304]
- shaking hands [p.331]
- smoking [p.354]

Produced by
- Otto Preminger Films
- Alpha Alpina

Pres. No.13

PRESIDENT
THOMAS ECKHART
“Agent X”
2015
Played by
John Shea

- arguing [p.55]
- briefing staff [p.96]
- gambling [p.131]
- in a meeting [p.204]
- in a video conference [p.222]
- looking shocked at a screen [p.270]
- on TV [p.297]
- screaming [p.327]
- with the Secret Service [p.423]

Produced by
- TNT Original Productions
- Beacon Pictures

Pres. No.14

PRESIDENT PHILLIPS
“Air Collision”
2012
Played by
Andy Clemence

- flying a plane [p.128]
- hugging his wife [p.175]
- reading files [p.312]
- scared [p.325]
- screaming [p.328]
- typing in a code [p.359]
- with his wife [p.413]

Produced by
- The Asylum

Pres. No.15

PRESIDENT
JAMES MARSHALL
“Air Force One”
1997
Played by
Harrison Ford

- boarding Air Force One [p.92]
- briefing staff [p.96]
- fighting [p.123]
- flying a plane [p.128]
- getting out of Air Force One, waving [p.142]
- giving a speech [p.151]
- greeting the military [p.163]
- hiding [p.171]
- hugging his family [p.175]
- in the office on board Air Force One [p.239]
- kissing [p.251]
- on board Air Force One [p.281]
- on the cell phone [p.285]
- on the telephone [p.290]
- reading files [p.313]
- saluting [p.322]
- sleeping [p.351]
- threatened with a weapon [p.374]
- washing his face [p.382]
- with a gun [p.399]
- with his daughter [p.407]
- with his wife [p.414]
- writing [p.433]

Produced by
- Columbia Pictures
- Beacon Communications
- Radiant Productions
- Beacon Pictures
- Etalon Film
- Touchstone Pictures

Pres. No.16

PRESIDENT
HARRIET FRANKLIN
“Airline Disaster”
2010
Played by
Meredith Baxter

- in a meeting [p.204]
- reading files [p.313]
- relieved [p.319]
- screaming [p.328]
- shocked [p.335]

Produced by
- The Asylum

Pres. No.17

THE PRESIDENT OF THE UNITED STATES OF AMERICA
“Amazing Grace and Chuck”
1987
Played by
Gregory Peck

- in a conversation [p.191]
- shaking hands [p.331]
- talking to a boy [p.359]

Produced by
- TriStar Pictures

Pres. No.18

PRESIDENT
JOSEPH STATON
“American Dreamz”
2006
Played by
Dennis Quaid

- eating in bed [p.121]
- getting out of the car [p.143]
- holding up a dog’s ears [p.173]
- in bed [p.227]
- in bed with his wife [p.230]
- lifting weights [p.255]
- looking at memories [p.262]
- meeting another politician [p.273]
- on TV [p.297]
- reading the newspaper [p.317]
- shaking hands [p.331]
- sitting on the desk in the Oval Office [p.343]
- watching TV [p.383]
- working in bed [p.427]

Produced by
- Universal Pictures
- Depth of Field

Pres. No.19

PRESIDENT
CHET ROOSEVELT
“Americathon”
1979
Played by
John Ritter

- addressing the nation on TV [p.52]
- at the inauguration [p.67]
- drinking through a straw [p.116]
- eating in bed [p.122]
- getting his nose licked [p.132]
- in a conversation [p.191]
- in a meeting [p.204]
- in bed with his mistress [p.229]
- in bed with his wife [p.230]
- in the newspaper [p.237]
- kissing [p.251]
- lifting weights [p.255]
- sitting on the desk in the Oval Office addressing the nation [p.347]
- watching TV [p.383]

Produced by
- Lorimar Television

Pres. No.20

THE PRESIDENT OF THE UNITED STATES OF AMERICA
“Austin Powers. The Spy Who Shagged Me”
1999
Played by
Tim Robbins

- hiding [p.171]
- in a meeting [p.204]
- in a meeting with the military [p.214]
- in a video conference [p.222]
- incredulous [p.247]
- laughing [p.254]

Produced by
- Eric’s Boy
- Moving Pictures
- Team Todd
- Lyons/Myers Productions

Pres.
No. 21

PRESIDENT
ADAIR T. MANNING
"Behind Enemy Lines 2: Axis of Evil"
2006
Played by
Peter Coyote

• awarding an officer [p. 69]
• behind the desk in the Oval Office [p. 72]
• being briefed [p. 81]
• in a meeting [p. 204]
• in a meeting with the military [p. 215]
• in a video conference [p. 222]
• in the Oval Office talking to the staff [p. 241]
• looking at military strategies [p. 263]
• meeting another politician [p. 273]
• shaking hands [p. 331]

Produced by
• Twentieth Century Fox

Pres.
No. 22

THE PRESIDENT OF THE UNITED STATES OF AMERICA
"Being There"
1979
Played by
Jack Warden

• addressing the nation [p. 52]
• at a funeral [p. 62]
• behind the desk in the Oval Office [p. 72]
• behind his desk in the Oval Office, talking to the staff [p. 77]
• giving a speech [p. 151]
• in a conversation [p. 191]
• in bed with his wife [p. 231]
• on the telephone [p. 290]
• on the telephone in bed [p. 294]
• on TV [p. 297]
• reading files [p. 313]
• shaking hands [p. 331]
• watching TV [p. 383]
• working out [p. 431]

Produced by
• Lorimar Productions

Pres.
No. 23

PRESIDENT
WILLIAM ALAN MOORE
"Big Game"
2014
Played by
Samuel L. Jackson

• bloodied [p. 88]
• boarding the Presidential Escape Pod [p. 94]
• eating [p. 114]
• fighting [p. 123]
• in a floating fridge [p. 198]
• in the crashed Air Force One [p. 233]
• in the newspaper [p. 237]
• in the office on board Air Force One [p. 239]
• injured [p. 247]
• on a tin can telephone [p. 281]
• reading the newspaper [p. 317]
• screaming [p. 328]
• shocked [p. 336]
• shooting [p. 338]
• threatened with a weapon [p. 374]
• with a dead body [p. 394]
• with a gun [p. 399]
• with a signal flare [p. 404]
• wrapped in a blanket [p. 433]

Produced by
• Subzero Film Entertainment
• Altitude Film Entertainment
• Egoli Tossell Film
• VisionPlus Fund
• Ketchup Entertainment
• Waterstone Entertainment
• Head Gear Films
• Metrol Technology
• Film House Germany
• Bavaria Film Partners

Pres.
No. 24

PRESIDENT
ARTHUR MOROSE
"By Dawn's Early Light"
1990
Played by
Martin Landau

• injured [p. 248]
• on the telephone [p. 290]
• reading files [p. 313]
• with the nuclear code [p. 419]

Produced by
• Paravision International
• HBO Pictures

Pres.
No. 25

THE PRESIDENT OF THE UNITED STATES OF AMERICA
"Canadian Bacon"
1995
Played by
Alan Alda

• addressing the nation on TV [p. 52]
• being briefed [p. 82]
• concerned [p. 105]
• drinking water [p. 117]
• eating chicken wings with another politician [p. 121]
• eating in bed [p. 122]
• frustrated [p. 129]
• getting out of the car [p. 143]
• giving a speech [p. 151]
• in a crisis situation [p. 196]
• in a meeting [p. 202]
• in a meeting room [p. 212]
• in the newspaper [p. 237]
• laughing [p. 254]
• meeting another politician [p. 273]
• on the red telephone [p. 288]
• on the telephone [p. 290]
• on TV [p. 297]
• reading files [p. 313]
• reading the newspaper [p. 317]
• scared [p. 325]
• sceaming [p. 328]
• shocked [p. 336]
• waving [p. 386]
• with a dead body [p. 394]

Produced by
• PolyGram Filmed Entertainment
• Propaganda Films
• David Brown Productions
• Maverick Picture Company

Pres.
No. 26

PRESIDENT
TOM KIMBALL
"Captain America"
1990
Played by
Ronny Cox

• addressing the nation on TV [p. 52]
• as a hostage [p. 57]
• behind his desk in the Oval Office, talking to the staff [p. 77]
• bloodied [p. 88]
• fighting [p. 124]
• fleeing [p. 126]
• hiding [p. 171]
• in the newspaper [p. 238]
• locked up [p. 257]
• on the cell phone [p. 285]
• on the telephone [p. 290]
• talking to a high-ranking officer [p. 360]
• threatened with a weapon [p. 374]
• with a gun [p. 399]
• with a superhero [p. 404]
• with feet on the table [p. 407]

Produced by
• Marvel Entertainment Group
• Jadran Film
• 21st Century Film Corporation

Pres.
No. 27

PRESIDENT
JACK CAHILL
"Chain of Command"
2000
Played by
Roy Scheider

• drinking coffee [p. 111]
• drinking alcohol [p. 113]
• in a meeting [p. 204]
• in a tracksuit [p. 219]
• on board Air Force One [p. 282]
• on the telephone [p. 290]
• threatened with a weapon [p. 375]
• wearing sunglasses [p. 389]

Produced by
• Cinetel Films
• Chain of Command Inc.

Pres.
No. 28

PRESIDENT
JAMES FOSTER
"Chasing Liberty"
2004
Played by
Mark Harmon

• arguing [p. 55]
• behind the desk in the Oval Office [p. 72]
• getting a promise from his daughter [p. 132]
• giving a press conference [p. 147]
• greeting guests at a banquet [p. 161]
• having breakfast [p. 165]
• hugging his daughter [p. 177]
• on the telephone [p. 290]
• on the telephone, reading files [p. 295]
• on TV [p. 297]
• playing Scrabble [p. 310]
• talking to his wife [p. 364]
• talking to his daughter [p. 366]
• waving [p. 386]
• with a dog [p. 396]
• with his daughter [p. 408]
• with his wife [p. 414]
• with the Secret Service [p. 424]

Produced by
• Alcon Entertainment

Pres.
No. 29

PRESIDENT BENNETT
"Clear and Present Danger"
1994
Played by
Donald Moffat

• angry [p. 54]
• at a funeral [p. 62]

• behind the desk in the Oval Office [p. 72]
• behind his desk in the Oval Office, talking to the staff [p. 77]
• broadcast on TV [p. 100]
• giving a press conference [p. 147]
• greeting the military [p. 163]
• in a conversation [p. 191]
• in a meeting [p. 204]
• on TV [p. 297]
• out for a hike [p. 302]
• shaking hands [p. 331]
• sitting on the desk in the Oval Office [p. 349]
• watching TV [p. 384]
• waving [p. 387]
• with a dog [p. 395]

Produced by
• Paramount Pictures
• Mace Neufeld Productions

Pres. No. 30

PRESIDENT MACKENZIE ALLEN
"Commander in Chief"
2005–2006
Played by
Geena Davis

• addressing the nation on TV [p. 52]
• behind the desk in the Oval Office [p. 72]
• behind her desk in the Oval Office, talking to the staff [p. 77]
• being briefed [p. 82]
• being sworn in [p. 86]
• briefing staff [p. 97]
• broadcast on TV [p. 100]
• drinking coffee [p. 112]
• frustrated [p. 129]
• getting out of the car [p. 143]
• giving a press conference [p. 147]
• having breakfast [p. 165]
• hugging her daughter [p. 177]
• in a conversation [p. 191]
• in a meeting [p. 204]
• in a meeting at the Oval Office [p. 208]
• in bed with her husband [p. 229]
• kissing [p. 251]
• looking at a screen [p. 260]
• on the telephone [p. 290]
• on TV [p. 297]
• reading files [p. 313]
• sitting on the desk in the Oval Office [p. 349]
• talking to her daughter [p. 366]
• thoughtful [p. 372]
• walking outside the Oval Office [p. 381]
• watching TV [p. 382]
• working late [p. 427]

Produced by
• Battleplan Productions
• Steven Bochco Productions
• Touchstone Television

Pres. No. 31

PRESIDENT RICHARD MARTINEZ
"Cory in the House"
2007–2008
Played by
John D'Aquino

• behind the desk in the Oval Office [p. 72]
• behind his desk in the Oval Office, talking to the staff [p. 77]
• giving a speech [p. 151]
• hugging his daughter [p. 178]
• in a bathrobe [p. 179]
• in a school class [p. 218]
• talking to his daughter [p. 366]
• with a balloon animal [p. 390]

Produced by
• It's a Laugh Productions
• Warren & Rinsler Productions

Pres. No. 32

PRESIDENT DEVORE
"Crisis"
2014
Played by
John Allen Nelson

• being briefed [p. 82]
• giving a speech [p. 151]
• lighting a candle in memory of hostages [p. 256]
• looking at a screen [p. 260]
• on a stage [p. 278]
• shaking hands [p. 331]
• with the Secret Service [p. 424]

Produced by
• Ravich/Shariat Productions
• 20th Century Fox Television
• National Broadcasting Company (NBC)

Pres. No. 33

PRESIDENT WILLIAM HARRISON MITCHEL
"Dave"
1993
Played by
Kevin Kline

• getting out of a helicopter [p. 138]
• giving a speech [p. 151]
• in a meeting [p. 204]
• in the hospital [p. 234]
• on TV [p. 297]
• sick in bed [p. 342]
• waving [p. 387]
• with a dog [p. 397]
• with his double [p. 410]

Produced by
• Northern Lights Entertainment
• Lauren Shuler Donner Productions

Pres. No. 34

PRESIDENT DAVE KOVIC
"Dave"
1993
Played by
Kevin Kline

• addressing Congress [p. 48]
• behind the desk in the Oval Office [p. 72]
• eating [p. 119]
• frustrated [p. 130]
• getting into a car [p. 135]
• giving a press conference [p. 148]
• giving a speech [p. 151]
• greeting a crowd [p. 158]
• greeting foreign politicians [p. 160]
• having dinner [p. 167]
• in a car [p. 184]
• in a kindergarten [p. 201]
• in a meeting [p. 204]
• in the kitchen [p. 236]
• in the shower [p. 244]
• looking at memories [p. 263]
• on the telephone [p. 290]
• on TV [p. 297]
• playing baseball [p. 306]
• riding on a pig [p. 321]
• shaking hands [p. 331]
• with a child [p. 392]
• with a dog [p. 397]
• with his double [p. 410]
• with robot arms [p. 415]
• with the Secret Service [p. 424]

Produced by
• Northern Lights Entertainment
• Lauren Shuler Donner Productions

Pres. No. 35

PRESIDENT GARY NANCE
"Dave"
1993
Played by
Ben Kingsley

• being sworn in [p. 86]

Produced by
• Northern Lights Entertainment
• Lauren Shuler Donner Productions

Pres. No. 36

PRESIDENT SEAN BRAYDEN
"DC's Legends of Tomorrow"
20[illegible]
Played by
Lucia Walters

• giving a speech [p. 148
• with a superhero [p. 405]

Produced by
• Berlanti Productions
• Bonanza Productions
• DC Entertainment
• Warner Bros. Television

Pres. No. 37

PRESIDENT TOM BECK
"Deep Impact"
1998
Played by
Morgan Freeman

• addressing the nation on TV [p. 52]
• behind the desk in the Oval Office [p. 72]
• being briefed [p. 82]
• broadcast on TV [p. 100]
• giving a press conference [p. 148]
• giving a speech [p. 151]
• in a restaurant kitchen [p. 216]
• in the Situation Room [p. 24[illegible]]
• looking at military strategies [p. 264]
• on TV [p. 297]
• talking to the press [p. 368]
• with the Secret Service [p. 424]

Produced by
• Paramount Pictures
• DreamWorks Pictures
• The Manhattan Project
• Zanuck/Brown Productions

Pres No. 33

PRESIDENT CORNELIUS MOSS
"Designated Survivor"
2016
Played by
Geoff Pierson

• addressing the nation on TV [p. 52]
• on TV [p. 297]

Produced by
• Kinberg Genre
• The Mark Gordon Company
• Baer Bores
• ABC Studios

Pres.
No.39

PRESIDENT
THOMAS ADAM
KIRKMAN
"Designated Survivor"
2016–2018
Played by
Kiefer Sutherland

- at the inauguration [p.67]
- behind the desk in the Oval Office [p.72]
- behind his desk in the Oval Office, talking to the staff [p.77]
- being briefed [p.82]
- being sworn in [p.86]
- broadcast on TV [p.100]
- getting out of the car [p.144]
- giving a speech [p.151]
- hugging his wife [p.176]
- in a conversation [p.191]
- in a crisis situation [p.196]
- in a meeting [p.204]
- in a meeting at the Oval Office [p.208]
- in a video conference with a terrorist [p.223]
- in the hospital [p.232]
- injured [p.248]
- in the Situation Room [p.245]
- looking at a screen [p.261]
- on a phone screen [p.276]
- on TV [p.297]
- praying [p.310]
- reading files [p.313]
- shot [p.340]
- signing files [p.342]
- sitting behind the desk addressing the nation [p.347]
- sitting on the desk in the Oval Office [p.350]
- speaking to a crowd with a megaphone [p.356]
- targeted by a gun [p.370]
- threatened with a weapon [p.375]
- watching TV [p.384]
- waving [p.387]
- with his wife [p.414]
- with the officer who is carrying the nuclear briefcase [p.421]
- with the Secret Service [p.424]
- working on a computer [p.429]

Produced by
- Kinberg Genre
- The Mark Gordon Company
- Baer Bones
- ABC Studios

Pres.
No.40

PRESIDENT
PETER MACLEISH
"Designated Survivor"
2017
Played by
Ashley Zukerman

- behind the desk in the Oval Office [p.72]
- giving a press conference [p.148]
- in the Situation Room [p.245]
- on TV [p.297]
- sitting outside the Oval Office [p.351]
- watching TV [p.384]

Produced by
- Kinberg Genre
- The Mark Gordon Company
- Baer Bones
- ABC Studios

Pres.
No.41

PRESIDENT
WALTER EMERSON
"Deterrence"
2000
Played by
Kevin Pollak

- broadcast on TV [p.100]
- on the telephone [p.290]
- on TV [p.297]
- playing pool [p.309]
- shaking hands [p.331]
- smoking [p.354]
- talking to a high-ranking officer [p.360]
- with the nuclear briefcase [p.416]

Produced by
- Battleplan Productions
- Moonstone Entertainment
- TF1 International

Pres.
No.42

PRESIDENT
MERKIN MUFFLEY
"Dr. Strangelove"
1964
Played by
Peter Sellers

- in a conversation [p.191]
- in a meeting [p.205]
- in a meeting with the military [p.215]
- on the telephone [p.290]
- talking to a high-ranking officer [p.360]

Produced by
- Columbia Pictures
- Hawk Films

Pres.
No.43

THE PRESIDENT OF THE UNITED STATES OF AMERICA
"Eagle Eye"
2008
Played by
Madison Mason

- addressing Congress [p.49]
- giving a speech [p.151]
- greeting a crowd [p.158]
- singing the national anthem [p.346]
- targeted by a gun [p.370]
- under fire [p.377]

Produced by
- DreamWorks
- Goldcrest Pictures
- KMP Film Invest
- Digital Image Associates
- K/O Paper Products

Pres.
No.44

THE PRESIDENT OF THE UNITED STATES OF AMERICA
"Escape from L.A."
1996
Played by
Cliff Robertson

- as a hologramm [p.56]
- being briefed [p.82]
- broadcast on TV [p.100]
- giving a speech [p.151]
- hiding [p.172]
- in a control center [p.188]
- in a conversation [p.191]
- looking shocked at a screen [p.270]
- on TV [p.271]
- smiling [p.352]
- talking to an inmate [p.361]
- thoughtful [p.372]
- with the military [p.415]

Produced by
- Paramount Pictures
- Rysher Entertainment

Pres.
No.45

THE PRESIDENT OF THE UNITED STATES OF AMERICA
"Escape from New York"
1981
Played by
Donald Pleasence

- as a hostage [p.57]
- boarding the Presidential Escape Pod [p.94]
- dressed as a woman [p.110]
- giving a speech [p.151]
- hiding [p.172]
- shaving [p.334]
- shooting [p.338]

Produced by
- Embassy Pictures
- International Film Investors
- Goldcrest Films International
- Major Studio Partners

Pres.
No.46

PRESIDENT
MATTHEW WILLIAMS
"Escape from the Planet of the Apes"
1971
Played by
William Windom

- behind the desk in the Oval Office [p.72]
- briefing staff [p.97]
- looking out the window of the Oval Office [p.269]
- on the telephone [p.290]
- reading files [p.313]
- smoking [p.354]

Produced by
- Twentieth Century Fox
- APJAC Productions

Pres.
No.47

PRESIDENT
JOHN FIELDS
"Executive Power"
1997
Played by
William Atherton

- behind his desk in the Oval Office, talking to the staff [p.77]
- in a conversation [p.191]
- on the telephone [p.291]
- signing files [p.343]
- smiling [p.352]
- with a dead body [p.394]

Produced by
- Initial Entertainment Group
- Naegele-Derrick Productions

Pres.
No.48

THE PRESIDENT OF THE UNITED STATES OF AMERICA
"Fail Safe"
1964
Played by
Henry Fonda

- briefing staff [p.97]
- helpless [p.169]
- in a conversation [p.191]
- in a meeting [p.205]
- in a meeting room [p.213]
- on the telephone [p.291]
- waiting [p.380]

• with the officer who is carrying the nuclear briefcase [p. 421]

Produced by
• Columbia Pictures

Pres. No. 49

PRESIDENT THOMAS MASON
"Falling Skies"
2013
Played by Noah Wyle

• behind his desk in the Oval Office, talking to the staff [p. 77]
• being briefed [p. 82]
• drinking alcohol [p. 113]
• in a meeting [p. 205]
• in the hospital [p. 234]
• reading files [p. 313]
• with a child [p. 392]
• with a gun [p. 400]
• with an alien [p. 402]
• working late [p. 428]

Produced by
• DreamWorks Television
• Amblin Television
• Invasion Productions
• TNT Original Productions

Pres. No. 50

PRESIDENT JOHN MACKENZIE
"First Daughter"
2004
Played by Michael Keaton

• behind his desk in the Oval Office, talking to the staff [p. 77]
• being briefed [p. 82]
• campaigning [p. 103]
• dancing [p. 106]
• eating cake [p. 120]
• getting out of a car [p. 144]
• giving a press conference [p. 148]
• giving a speech [p. 151]
• greeting guests at a banquet [p. 161]
• in a meeting [p. 205]
• on a sign [p. 277]
• on stage [p. 279]
• on the telephone [p. 291]
• reading files [p. 313]
• with his daughter [p. 408]
• with his wife [p. 414]

Produced by
• Regency Enterprises
• New Regency Pictures
• Davis Entertainment
• Spirit Dance Entertainment
• Epsilon Motion Pictures

Pres. No. 51

PRESIDENT JONATHAN HAYES
"First Daughter"
1999
Played by Gregory Harrison

• helpless [p. 170]
• hugging his daughter [p. 178]
• in a video conference with a terrorist [p. 223]
• looking shocked at a screen [p. 271]
• on the telephone [p. 291]
• reading files [p. 313]
• talking to his daughter [p. 367]
• targeted by a gun [p. 370]

Produced by
• TBS Superstation
• Columbia TriStar Television
• Lions Gate Television
• Mandalay Television

Pres. No. 52

PRESIDENT JONATHAN HAYES
"First Shot"
2002
Played by Gregory Harrison

• briefing staff [p. 97]
• giving a speech [p. 152]
• in the hospital [p. 235]
• in the newspaper [p. 238]
• in the Oval Office talking to the staff [p. 242]
• on the telephone [p. 291]
• on TV [p. 298]
• talking to his wife [p. 364]
• talking to his daughter [p. 367]
• under fire [p. 378]
• with his daughter [p. 409]
• with his family [p. 411]

Produced by
• Columbia TriStar Television
• Lions Gate Television
• Mandalay Entertainment
• Sony Pictures Television International
• TBS Superstation

Pres. No. 53

PRESIDENT JONATHAN HAYES
"First Target"
2000
Played by Gregory Harrison

• as a hostage [p. 57]
• behind his desk in the Oval Office, talking to his staff [p. 77]
• fighting [p. 124]
• giving a speech [p. 152]
• having breakfast [p. 165]
• having dinner [p. 167]
• hiding [p. 172]
• in a cable railway [p. 183]
• in the Oval Office talking to the staff [p. 242]
• on the telephone [p. 291]
• screaming [p. 328]
• shaking hands [p. 331]
• signing files [p. 343]
• under fire [p. 378]
• with a gun [p. 391]

Produced by
• Columbia TriStar International Television
• KirchMedia
• Lions Gate Television
• Mandalay Sports Entertainment
• Mandalay Television
• Province of British Columbia Production Services Tax Credit

Pres. No. 54

THE PRESIDENT OF THE UNITED STATES OF AMERICA
"G.I. Joe 1"
2009
Played by Jonathan Pryce

• addressing the nation on TV [p. 52]
• as a hostage [p. 58]
• as an alien [p. 59]
• dancing [p. 106]
• giving a speech [p. 152]
• meeting another politician [p. 274]
• in a meeting with the military [p. 215]
• on TV [p. 271]
• shaking hands [p. 331]
• shot [p. 340]
• talking to a boy [p. 359]
• threatened with a weapon [p. 375]
• with a gun [p. 390]
• with a knife [p. 301]
• with an alien [p. 402]
• with his double [p. 410]
• with the nuclear briefcase [p. 417]

Produced by
• Paramount Pictures
• Spyglass Entertainment
• Hasbro
• Di Bonaventura Pictures
• Digital Image Associates

Pres. No. 55

THE PRESIDENT OF THE UNITED STATES OF AMERICA
"G.I. Joe 2"
2013
Played by Jonathan Pryce

• behind the desk in the Oval Office [p. 72]
• behind his desk in the Oval Office, talking to the staff [p. 77]
• in the Oval Office talking to the staff [p. 242]
• in the Situation Room [p. 245]
• looking out the window of the Oval Office [p. 269]
• shocked [p. 336]
• with feet on the table [p. 407]

Produced by
• Paramount Pictures
• Metro-Goldwyn-Mayer
• Skydance Media
• Hasbro
• Di Bonaventura Pictures
• Saints LA
• Spyglass Entertainment

Pres. No. 56

PRESIDENT JUDSON HAMMOND
"Gabriel Over the White House"
1933
Played by Walter Huston

• addressing Congress [p. 49]
• being sworn in [p. 87]
• dead [p. 108]
• getting out of a car [p. 144]
• giving a speech [p. 152]
• greeting guests at a banquet [p. 161]
• in a bathrobe [p. 179]
• in a car [p. 184]
• in a conversation [p. 191]
• in a meeting [p. 205]
• in bed [p. 227]
• in the Oval Office talking to the staff [p. 242]
• injured [p. 248]
• reading files [p. 313]
• shaking hands [p. 331]
• signing files [p. 343]
• working late [p. 428]

Produced by
• Metro-Goldwyn-Mayer

Pres.
No.57

PRESIDENT
ANDREW PALMA
"Geostorm"
2017
Played by
Andy Garcia

- boarding Air Force One [p.92]
- campaigning [p.103]
- getting out of a helicopter [p.138]
- getting out of a car [p.144]
- giving a speech [p.152]
- in a car [p.184]
- in a crisis situation [p.197]
- in a meeting [p.205]
- in a video conference [p.222]
- looking shocked at a screen [p.271]
- screaming [p.328]
- threatened with a weapon [p.375]
- under fire [p.378]

Produced by
- Warner Bros.
- Electric Entertainment
- RatPac-Dune Entertainment
- Skydance Media
- Stereo D
- Twisted Media

Pres.
No.58

PRESIDENT
RICHARD GRAVES
"Graves"
2016–2017
Played by
Nick Nolte

- drinking alcohol [p.114]
- giving a speech [p.152]
- giving someone the finger [p.156]
- in a car [p.185]
- looking in the mirror [p.266]
- on TV [p.298]
- shaking hands [p.331]
- sitting on the desk in the Oval Office [p.350]
- smoking [p.355]
- waving [p.387]
- with a knife [p.401]
- working on a computer [p.430]
- working out [p.431]

Produced by
- Lionsgate Television

Pres.
No.59

PRESIDENT
MAYS GILLIAM
"Head of State"
2003
Played by
Chris Rock

- as DJ [p.56]
- campaigning [p.103]
- dancing [p.106]
- giving a speech [p.152]
- in a church [p.187]
- in a conversation [p.191]
- in a kindergarten [p.192]
- in bed [p.227]
- kissing [p.252]
- looking in the mirror [p.266]
- on stage [p.279]
- on the telephone [p.291]
- on TV [p.298]
- shaking hands [p.331]
- shocked [p.337]
- talking to the press [p.368]
- watching TV [p.384]
- with a child [p.392]

Produced by
- Warner Bros.
- Electric Entertainment
- RatPac-Dune Entertainment
- Skydance Media
- Stereo D
- Twisted Media

Pres.
No.60

PRESIDENT
NATHAN PETRELLI
"Heroes"
2006–2010
Played by
Adrian Pasdar

- in the kitchen [p.236]
- talking to the press [p.369]
- with the secret sevice [p.424]

Produced by
- Tailwind Productions
- NBC Universal Television
- Universal Media Studios

Pres.
No.61

PRESIDENT
ELIZABETH KEANE
"Homeland"
2017
Played by
Elizabeth Marvel

- behind the desk in the Oval Office [p.72]
- being briefed [p.82]
- broadcast on TV [p.100]
- drinking coffee [p.112]
- drinking water [p.117]
- fleeing [p.126]
- getting out of a helicopter [p.138]
- getting out of a car [p.144]
- in a conversation [p.191]
- in a helicopter [p.198]
- on the cell phone [p.286]
- reading files [p.313]
- screaming [p.328]
- signing files [p.344]
- talking to the press [p.369]

Produced by
- Teakwood Lane Productions
- Cherry Pie Productions
- Keshet Broadcasting
- Fox 21
- Showtime Networks

Pres.
No.62

PRESIDENT MORSE
"Homeland"
2017
Played by Alan Dale

- giving a speech [p.152]
- on TV [p.271]

Produced by
- Teakwood Lane Productions
- Cherry Pie Productions
- Keshet Broadcasting
- Fox 21
- Showtime Networks

Pres.
No.63

PRESIDENT
PAUL KINCAID
"Hostages"
2013–2014
Played by
James Naughton

- giving a speech [p.152]
- in a car [p.185]
- in the hospital [p.235]
- on TV [p.198]

Produced by
- Jerry Bruckheimer Television
- Nana 10
- Warner Bros. Television

Pres.
No.64

PRESIDENT
THOMAS BENSON
"Hot Shots! Part Deux"
1993
Played by
Lloyd Bridges

- at a banquet [p.60]
- being briefed [p.82]
- diving [p.110]
- fighting with a lightsaber [p.125]
- getting out of a helicopter [p.139]
- giving a speech [p.152]
- greeting a crowd [p.159]
- in a conversation [p.192]
- looking at a globe [p.258]
- offering candies [p.275]
- on board Air Force One [p.282]
- sharpening a pencil in his ear [p.334]
- signing files [p.344]
- smoking [p.355]
- vomiting [p.380]
- washing dentures in the glass of another politician [p.382]
- waving [p.387]
- with a Lincoln bust [p.391]
- with a child [p.331]
- with dentures [p.406]
- with his wife [p.414]

Produced by
- Twentieth Century Fox

Pres.
No.65

PRESIDENT
MICHEL GILL
"House of Cards"
2013
Played by
Garrett Walker

- addressing Congress [p.49]
- at the inauguration [p.67]
- behind the desk in the Oval Office [p.73]
- being sworn in [p.87]
- broadcast on TV [p.100]
- drinking alcohol [p.114]
- giving a press conference [p.148]
- giving a speech [p.152]
- in a conversation [p.192]
- in a meeting at the Oval Office [p.208]
- in the Oval Office talking to the staff [p.242]
- on TV [p.298]
- reading files [p.313]
- shaking hands [p.332]
- signing files [p.344]
- sitting on the desk in the Oval Office [p.350]
- waving [p.387]

Produced by
- Media Rights Capital (MRC)
- Netflix
- Panic Pictures (II)
- Trigger Street Productions

Pres.
No.66

PRESIDENT
FRANCIS J.UNDERWOOD
"House of Cards"
2013–2017
Played by
Kevin Spacey

- at a banquet [p.60]
- at a funeral [p.62]
- at a graveyard [p.64]
- at a state reception [p.65]
- behind the desk in the Oval Office [p.73]
- being briefed [p.82]
- drinking alcohol [p.114]
- giving a speech [p.152]
- giving a press conference [p.148]
- hiding [p.172]
- in a bathrobe [p.180]

• in a conversation [p.192]
• in a meeting [p.205]
• in a meeting at the Oval Office [p.209]
• in bed [p.228]
• in the kitchen [p.236]
• in the newspaper [p.238]
• looking out of the window of the Oval Office [p.269]
• meeting another politician [p.274]
• on the telephone [p.291]
• on TV [p.298]
• shaking hands [p.332]
• singing [p.345]
• smoking [p.355]
• talking to his wife [p.364]
• with his wife [p.414]
• working [p.425]
• working on a computer [p.430]

Produced by
• Media Rights Capital (MRC)
• Netflix
• Panic Pictures (II)
• Trigger Street Productions

Pres.
No.67

PRESIDENT
CLAIRE UNDERWOOD
"House of Cards"
2017
Played by
Robin Wright

• behind her desk in the Oval Office, talking to the staff [p.77]
• being sworn in [p.87]
• giving a press conference [p.148]
• giving a speech [p.152]
• in the Situation Room [p.246]

Produced by
• Media Rights Capital (MRC)
• Netflix
• Panic Pictures (II)
• Trigger Street Productions

Pres.
No.68

PRESIDENT
DWAYNE ELIZONDO
MOUNTAIN DEW
HERBERT CAMACHO
"Idiocracy"
2006
Played by
Terry Crews

• addressing Congress [p.50]
• giving someone the finger [p.157]
• in a meeting at the Oval Office [p.209]
• in the Oval Office talking to the staff [p.242]
• riding a motorbike [p.320]
• singing [p.345]
• with a gun [p.400]

Produced by
• Twentieth Century Fox
• Ternion Pictures
• Major Studio Partners

Pres.
No.69

PRESIDENT
JOE BAUERS
"Idiocracy"
2006
Played by
Joe Bauers

• addressing Congress [p.50]
• giving a speech [p.152]
• giving someone the finger [p.157]
• on TV [p.298]
• with his family [p.411]

Produced by
• Twentieth Century Fox
• Ternion Pictures
• Major Studio Partners

Pres.
No.70

THE PRESIDENT OF THE UNITED STATES OF AMERICA
"In the Line of Fire"
1993
Played by
Jim Curley

• at a state reception [p.65]
• campaigning [p.104]
• drinking alcohol [p.114]
• fleeing [p.125]
• getting out of Air Force One [p.140]
• getting out of Air Force One, waving [p.142]
• getting out of the car [p.144]
• giving a speech [p.153]
• greeting a crowd [p.159]
• greeting guests at a banquet [p.162]
• hiding [p.172]
• in a car [p.185]
• in a restaurant kitchen [p.216]
• in the newspaper [p.238]
• shaking hands [p.332]
• threatened with a weapon [p.375]
• under fire [p.379]

Produced by
• Columbia Pictures
• Castle Rock Entertainment

Pres.
No.71

PRESIDENT
THOMAS J. WHITMORE
"Independence Day"
1996
Played by
Bill Pullman

• being briefed [p.82]
• boarding a helicopter [p.90]
• boarding Air Force One [p.92]
• fleeing [p.127]
• flying a plane [p.128]
• getting out of a helicopter [p.139]
• giving a press conference [p.148]
• having breakfast [p.166]
• hugging his daughter [p.178]
• in a bathrobe [p.180]
• in a conversation [p.192]
• in a lab [p.202]
• in a meeting [p.205]
• in a meeting at the Oval Office [p.209]
• in a video conference [p.222]
• in the Oval Office talking to the staff [p.242]
• kissing [p.252]
• looking at a spaceship [p.262]
• looking at military strategies [p.264]
• on board Air Force One [p.282]
• on the telephone [p.291]
• reading the newspaper [p.318]
• saluting [p.322]
• screaming [p.328]
• shocked [p.337]
• speaking to a crowd with a megaphone [p.356]
• talking to his wife [p.365]
• with a dead body [p.395]
• with an alien [p.402]
• with his daughter [p.309]
• with his family [p.411]
• with the officer who is carrying the nuclear briefcase [p.422]

Produced by
• Twentieth Century Fox
• Centropolis Entertainment

Pres.
No.72

PRESIDENT
ELIZABETH LANFORD
"Independence Day Resurgence"
2016
Played by
Sela Ward

• being briefed [p.82]
• boarding a helicopter [p.90]
• fleeing [p.127]
• getting out of a helicopter [p.139]
• giving a speech [p.153]
• in a video conference [p.222]
• looking at a screen [p.261]
• looking shocked at a screen [p.27[illegible]]
• on TV [p.298]
• reading files [p.314]
• saluting [p.322]

Produced by
• Twentieth Century Fox
• TSG Entertainment
• Centropolis Entertainment
• Electric Entertainment
• Moving Picture Company
• Twisted Media

Pres.
No.73

PRESIDENT
JOSHUA T. ADAMSE
"Independence Day Resurgence"
2016
Played by
William Fichtner

• being briefed [p.82]
• being sworn in [p.87]
• in a conversation [p.192]
• with the military [p.416]

Produced by
• Twentieth Century Fox
• TSG Entertainment
• Centropolis Entertainment
• Electric Entertainment
• Moving Picture Company
• Twisted Media

Pres.
No.74

PRESIDENT
MATTHEW ELLIS
"Iron Man 3"
2013
Played by
William Sadler

• being briefed [p.83]
• boarding Air Force One [p.93]
• giving a press conference [p.148]
• hiding [p.172]
• in a meeting [p.205]
• in a video conference with a terrorist [p.223]
• on a sign [p.259]
• on the cell phone [p.28[illegible]]
• on TV [p.298]
• saluting [p.323]
• thoughtful [p.372]
• with a superhero [p.405]

Produced by
• Marvel Studios
• Paramount Pictures
• DMG Entertainment

• Illusion Entertainment
• Taurus Studios

Pres.
No.75
PRESIDENT LESLIE MCCLOUD
"Kisses for My President"
1964
Played by Polly Bergen
• behind the desk in the Oval Office [p.73]
• being briefed [p.83]
• in a meeting [p.205]
• kissing [p.252]
• reading files [p.323]
• talking to her husband [p.362]
Produced by
• Warner Bros.
• Pearlayne

Pres.
No.76
PRESIDENT GERALD FITZHUGH
"Left Behind: World at War"
2005
Played by Louis Gossett, Jr.
• behind the desk in the Oval Office [p.73]
• being briefed [p.83]
• drinking alcohol [p.114]
• hiding [p.172]
• in a car [p.185]
• in a conversation [p.192]
• in a meeting at the Oval Office [p.209]
• looking at military strategies [p.264]
• looking shocked at a screen [p.271]
• on the telephone [p.291]
• talking to an inmate [p.361]
• threatened with a weapon [p.375]
• with a gun [p.391]
Produced by
• Cloud Ten Pictures
• Columbia Pictures

Pres.
No.77
PRESIDENT REGINALD J. PRIEST
"Lexx"
2000
Played by Rolf Kanies
• behind his desk in the Oval Office, talking to the staff [p.78]
• being sworn in [p.87]
• in a meeting at the Oval Office [p.209]
• in the Oval Office talking to the staff [p.242]
• on the telephone [p.291]
• on TV [p.298]
Produced by
• Chum Television
• ZenHQ Films

Pres.
No.78
PRESIDENT JEFF DAVISON
"Lexx"
2001
Played by Chas Lawther
• behind the desk in the Oval Office [p.73]
• helpless [p.170]
• thoughtful [p.373]
• watching TV [p.384]
Produced by
• Chum Television
• ZenHQ Films

Pres.
No.79
PRESIDENT BENJAMIN ASHER
"London Has Fallen"
2016
Played by Aaron Eckhart
• as a hostage [p.58]
• behind the desk in the Oval Office [p.73]
• being briefed [p.83]
• bloodied [p.88]
• boarding a helicopter [p.90]
• fleeing [p.127]
• getting into a car [p.136]
• getting out of a helicopter [p.139]
• getting out of Air Force One [p.140]
• getting out of the car [p.144]
• hiding [p.172]
• in a car [p.185]
• in a video conference [p.222]
• in a video conference with a terrorist [p.224]
• in the Oval Office talking to the staff [p.242]
• looking out the window of the Oval Office [p.269]
• on the telephone [p.291]
• on TV [p.298]
• shaking hands [p.332]
• sitting on the desk in the Oval Office [p.350]
• under fire [p.379]
• with a crashed helicopter [p.393]
• working out [p.431]
Produced by
• Millennium Films G-BASE
• Caffeination
• LHF Film
• Nu Boyana Film Studios

Pres.
No.80
THE PRESIDENT OF THE UNITED STATES OF AMERICA
"Love Actually"
2003
Played by Billy Bob Thornton
• at a state reception [p.65]
• getting out of the car [p.144]
• giving a press conference [p.148]
• in a conversation [p.192]
• in a meeting [p.205]
• meeting another politician [p.274]
• waving [p.387]
Produced by
• Universal Pictures
• StudioCanal
• Working Title Films
• DNA Films

Pres.
No.81
THE PRESIDENT OF THE UNITED STATES OF AMERICA
"Machete Kills"
2013
Played by Charlie Sheen
• behind the desk in the Oval Office [p.73]
• campaigning [p.104]
• drinking alcohol [p.114]
• reading files [p.314]
• smoking [p.355]
• waving [p.387]
• with a gun [p.400]
Produced by
• AR Films
• Aldamisa Entertainment
• 1821 Pictures
• Quick Draw Productions
• Demarest Films
• Overnight Films

Pres.
No.82
PRESIDENT CONRAD DALTON
"Madam Secretary"
2014
Played by Keith Carradine
• being briefed [p.83]
• broadcast on TV [p.100]
• drinking alcohol [p.114]
• getting out of the car [p.144]
• in a conversation [p.192]
• in a meeting [p.205]
• in a meeting at the Oval Office [p.209]
• in the Situation Room [p.246]
• on TV [p.299]
• with a gun [p.400]
Produced by
• Barbara Hall Productions
• Revelations Entertainment
• CBS Television Studios

Pres.
No.83
PRESIDENT ELIZABETH MCCORD
"Madam Secretary"
2015
Played by Téa Leoni
• behind her desk in the Oval Office, talking to the staff [p.78]
• being briefed [p.83]
• being sworn in [p.87]
• getting dressed [p.133]
• in a conversation [p.192]
• in a meeting [p.205]
• in a meeting at the Oval Office [p.209]
• in the Oval Office talking to the staff [p.242]
• signing files [p.344]
• with the officer who is carrying the nuclear briefcase [p.422]
• working [p.425]
Produced by
• Barbara Hall Productions
• Revelations Entertainment
• CBS Television Studios

Pres.
No.84
PRESIDENT TOM DOBBS
"Man of the Year"
2006
Played by Robin Williams
• addressing Congress [p.50]
• behind the desk in the Oval Office [p.73]
• behind his desk in the Oval Office, talking to the staff [p.78]
• broadcast on TV [p.100]
• giving a speech [p.153]
• in a car [p.185]
• in a conversation [p.192]
• in a restaurant kitchen [p.216]
• in the newspaper [p.238]
• on board Air Force One [p.283]
• on the cell phone [p.286]
• on the telephone [p.291]
• on TV [p.299]
• shaking hands [p.332]
• singing [p.345]
• talking to the press [p.369]
Produced by
• Universal Pictures

• Morgan Creek Entertainment

Pres.
No. 85

PRESIDENT KELLOGG
"Man of the Year"
2006
Played by
David Nichols

• on a stage [p. 279]

Produced by
• Universal Pictures
• Morgan Creek Entertainment

Pres.
No. 86

PRESIDENT JAMES DALE
"Mars Attacks!"
1996
Played by
Jack Nicholson

• behind the desk in the Oval Office [p. 73]
• behind his desk in the Oval Office, talking to the staff [p. 78]
• being briefed [p. 83]
• broadcast on TV [p. 100]
• dead [p. 103]
• frustrated [p. 130]
• giving a press conference [p. 148]
• having dinner [p. 168]
• in a meeting [p. 205]
• in a meeting with the military [p. 215]
• in bed with his wife [p. 231]
• on the red telephone [p. 287]
• on TV [p. 299]
• reading files [p. 314]
• scared [p. 325]
• screaming [p. 328]
• shaking hands [p. 332]
• signing files [p. 344]
• sitting behind the desk addressing the nation [p. 347]
• threatened with a weapon [p. 375]
• watching TV [p. 384]
• with an alien [p. 403]
• working [p. 425]

Produced by
• Tim Burton Productions
• Warner Bros.

Pres.
No. 87

PRESIDENT DAVID ALEXANDER
"Megiddo. The Omega Code 2"
2001
Played by
Michael Biehn

• boarding a helicopter [p. 91]
• fleeing [p. 127]
• getting out of the car [p. 144]
• hiding [p. 172]
• in a helicopter [p. 199]
• in a meeting [p. 206]
• locked up [p. 257]
• looking at military strategies [p. 265]
• looking shocked at a screen [p. 271]
• on TV [p. 299]
• screaming [p. 328]
• shaking hands [p. 332]
• threatened with a weapon [p. 375]
• watching TV [p. 384]
• with a gun [p. 400]

Produced by
• Code Productions
• Gener8Xion Entertainment
• Infinity Omnimedia
• TBN Films

Pres.
No. 88

PRESIDENT RICHARD BENSON
"Megiddo. The Omega Code 2"
2001
Played by
R. Lee Ermey

• in a video conference [p. 222]
• on board Air Force One [p. 283]
• reading files [p. 314]
• smiling [p. 352]

Produced by
• Code Productions
• Gener8Xion Entertainment
• Infinity Omnimedia
• TBN Films

Pres.
No. 89

PRESIDENT HELEN TYLER
"Modus"
2015
Played by
Kim Cattrall

• being briefed [p. 83]
• drinking coffee [p. 112]
• getting out of Air Force One, waving [p. 142]
• getting out of the car [p. 144]
• in a car [p. 185]
• looking at a painting [p. 259]
• on TV [p. 299]
• reading files [p. 314]

Produced by
• C More
• TV4
• Miso Film Sverige
• Zweites Deutsches Fernsehen
• Nadcon Film
• TV2 Norge
• TV2 Danmark
• Ríkisút-varpið-Sjónvarp
• Lumière
• Fremantle Media International
• MEDIA Programme of the European Union
• Svenska Filminstitutet
• Nordisk Film- & TV-Fond

Pres.
No. 90

PRESIDENT SAMUEL ARTHUR TRESCH
"Mr. President"
1987–1988
Played by
George C. Scott

• behind the desk in the Oval Office [p. 73]
• behind his desk in the Oval Office, talking to the staff [p. 78]
• briefing staff [p. 97]
• gambling [p. 131]
• in a meeting at the Oval Office [p. 209]
• reading files [p. 314]

Produced by
• Carson Productions

Pres.
No. 91

PRESIDENT JACK NEIL
"Murder at 1600"
1997
Played by Ronny Cox

• behind his desk in the Oval Office, talking to the staff [p. 78]
• being briefed [p. 83]
• in a conversation [p. 192]
• in a meeting at the Oval Office [p. 209]
• on the telephone [p. 291]
• playing baseball [p. 306]
• waving [p. 387]

Produced by
• Warner Bros.
• Regency Enterprises
• 1600 Limited Partnership
• Kopelson Entertainment

Pres.
No. 92

PRESIDENT GEORGE RICHMOND
"My Date with the President's Daughter"
1998
Played by
Dabney Coleman

• behind his desk in the Oval Office, talking to the staff [p. 78]
• frustrated [p. 130]
• giving a speech [p. 156]
• having breakfast [p. 166]
• hugging his wife [p. 176]
• hugging his daughter [p. 178]
• in a car [p. 185]
• locked up [p. 257]
• on a sign [p. 277]
• on TV [p. 299]
• playing golf [p. 307]
• reading files [p. 314]
• reading the newspaper [p. 318]
• shaking hands [p. 332]
• talking to a boy [p. 359]
• with his wife [p. 414]

Produced by
• Katz Entertainment
• Pacific Motion Pictures
• Walt Disney Television

Pres.
No. 93

PRESIDENT RUSSELL KRAMER
"My Fellow Americans"
1996
Played by
Jack Lemmon

• campaigning [p. 104]
• giving a speech [p. 155]
• in a helicopter [p. 201]
• in bed [p. 230]
• on board Air Force One [p. 235]
• out for a hike [p. 304]
• riding a horse [p. 321]

Produced by
• Peters Entertainment
• Storyline Entertainment

Pres.
No. 94

PRESIDENT MATT DOUGLAS
"My Fellow Americans"
1996
Played by
James Garner

• campaigning [p. 104]
• getting dressed [p. 133]
• giving a speech [p. 153]
• in a car [p. 185]
• in the bathroom [p. 232]
• on board Air Force One [p. 283]
• on the telephone [p. 292]
• riding a motorbike [p. 320]
• saluting [p. 323]

Produced by
• Peters Entertainment
• Storyline Entertainment

Pres.
No. 95

PRESIDENT WILLIAM HANEY
"My Fellow Americans"
1996
Played by
Dan Aykroyd

• giving a speech [p. 153]
• greeting a crowd [p. 159]
• in a conversation [p. 192]
• on TV [p. 299]
• photographed by the press [p. 304]
• playing golf [p. 308]

• watching TV [p.384]
• working out [p.432]

Produced by
• Peters Entertainment
• Storyline Entertainme

Pres.
No.96

PRESIDENT KATHLEEN SPENCER
"Nikita"
2011–2013
Played by
Michelle Nolden

• as a hostage [p.58]
• behind the desk in the Oval Office [p.73]
• behind her desk in the Oval Office, talking to the staff [p.78]
• dead [p.109]
• in a conversation [p.192]
• in a meeting at the Oval Office [p.209]
• locked up [p.261]
• on the telephone [p.292]
• on TV [p.299]
• working [p.426]

Produced by
• Sesfonstein Productions
• Wonderland Sound and Vision
• Warner Bros. Television
• Nikita Films

Pres.
No.97

PRESIDENT LYMAN
"Nothing but the Truth"
2008
Played by
Scott Williamson

• in a car [p.185]
• injured [p.249]

Produced by
• Yari Film Group
• Battleplan Productions

Pres.
No.98

PRESIDENT BENJAMIN ASHER
"Olympus Has Fallen"
2013
Played by
Aaron Eckhart

• as a hostage [p.58]
• being briefed [p.83]
• bloodied [p.89]
• briefing staff [p.97]
• getting dressed [p.133]
• giving a press conference [p.148]
• giving a speech [p.153]
• in a car [p.185]
• in a conversation [p.192]
• in a meeting at the Oval Office [p.209]
• in a video conference with a terrorist [p.224]
• injured [p.249]
• kissing [p.252]
• looking at a screen [p.261]
• meeting another politician [p.274]
• on TV [p.299]
• screaming [p.328]
• talking to his son [p.363]
• threatened with a weapon [p.375]
• with a gun [p.400]
• with his wife [p.414]

Produced by
• Millennium Films (presents)
• Millennium Films (as Nu Image)
• G-BASE
• Caffeination
• FortyFour Studios
• West Coast Film Partners

Pres.
No.99

PRESIDENT ALLAN TRUMBULL
"Olympus Has Fallen"
2013
Played by
Morgan Freeman

• addressing the nation on TV [p.52]
• being briefed [p.83]
• frustrated [p.130]
• helpless [p.170]
• in a meeting [p.206]
• looking at a screen [p.261]
• looking shocked at a screen [p.271]
• on TV [p.299]
• watching TV [p.384]
• with the officer who is carrying the nuclear briefcase [p.422]

Produced by
• Millennium Films (presents)
• Millennium Films (as Nu Image)
• G-BASE
• Caffeination
• FortyFour Studios
• West Coast Film Partners

Pres.
No.100

PRESIDENT PAUL GARCETTI
"Political Animals"
2012
Played by
Adrian Pasdar

• addressing the nation on TV [p.52]
• behind the desk in the Oval Office [p.73]
• behind his desk in the Oval Office, talking to the staff [p.78]
• being briefed [p.83]
• briefing staff [p.97]
• broadcast on TV [p.100]
• campaigning [p.104]
• dancing [p.107]
• frustrated [p.130]
• in a conversation [p.193]
• in a meeting [p.206]
• in a meeting at the Oval Office [p.209]
• in the Situation Room [p.246]
• reading files [p.314]
• smiling [p.351]
• talking to his son [p.363]

Produced by
• Berlanti Productions
• Laurence Mark Productions
• Warner Horizon Television

Pres.
No.101

THE PRESIDENT OF THE UNITED STATES OF AMERICA
"President Under Siege"
2016
Played by
Saskia Reeves

• at a banquet [p.61]
• at a state reception [p.66]
• behind the desk in the Oval Office [p.73]
• fleeing [p.127]
• getting out of Air Force One, waving [p.142]
• hiding [p.172]
• in a car [p.185]
• in a conversation [p.193]
• on the telephone [p.292]
• photographed by the press [p.304]
• shaking hands [p.332]
• shocked [p.337]
• threatened with a weapon [p.375]
• waving [p.387]

Produced by
• FBO
• Millstreet Films
• Woestijnvis

Pres.
No.102

PRESIDENT JACK STANTON
"Primary Colors"
1998
Played by
John Travolta

• campaigning [p.104]
• dancing [p.107]
• giving a speech [p.153]
• in a car [p.185]
• in the bathroom [p.233]
• on TV [p.299]
• reading files [p.314]

Produced by
• Award Entertainment
• British Broadcasting Corporation
• H2L Media Group
• Hollywood Licensing Group
• Icarus Productions
• Marubeni
• Mutual Film Company
• Tele München Fernseh Produktionsgesellschaft
• Toho-Towa
• UGC PH
• Universal Pictures

Pres.
No.103

PRESIDENT RICHARD MILLS
"Prison Break"
2005
Played by
Daniel J. Travanti

• in a conversation [p.193]
• on TV [p.299]

Produced by
• Adelstein-Parouse Productions
• Dawn Olmstead Productions
• Adelstein Productions
• Original Television
• 20th Century Fox Television
• Original Film
• One Light Road Productions
• Prison Break Productions

Pres.
No.104

PRESIDENT CAROLINE REYNOLDS
"Prison Break"
2006
Played by
Patricia Wettig

• being sworn in [p.87]
• briefing staff [p.97]
• drinking alcohol [p.114]
• getting out of the car [p.144]
• giving a press conference [p.148]
• giving a speech [p.153]
• greeting a crowd [p.159]
• in a conversation [p.193]
• in a restaurant kitchen [p.217]
• on a sign [p.278]
• on the cell phone [p.287]
• on TV [p.299]
• reading files [p.314]
• targeted by a gun [p.371]
• working [p.426]
• working late [p.428]

Produced by
• Adelstein-Parouse Productions
• Dawn Olmstead Productions
• Adelstein Productions
• Original Television
• 20th Century Fox Television
• Original Film

- One Light Road Productions
- Prison Break Productions

Pres.
No.105

PRESIDENT MIMEO
"Putney Swope"
1969
Played by Pepi Hermine

- in a conversation [p.193]
- in bed with his wife [p.231]
- kissing [p.252]
- on the telephone [p.292]
- on the telephone in bed [p.294]
- shaking hands [p.332]

Produced by
- Herald Productions (II)

Pres.
No.106

PRESIDENT TODD
"Quantico"
2016
Played by
Danny Johnson

- broadcast on TV [p.100]
- fleeing [p.127]
- giving a speech [p.153]

Produced by
- The Mark Gordon Company
- Random Acts
- Entertainment
- ABC Studios
- Master Key Production

Pres.
No.107

PRESIDENT CLAIRE HAAS
"Quantico"
2017
Played by
Marcia Cross

- addressing the nation on TV [p.52]
- briefing staff [p.97]
- giving a speech [p.153]
- hugging her son [p.174]
- in a conversation [p.193]
- in a meeting room [p.213]
- on TV [p.299]

Produced by
- The Mark Gordon Company
- Random Acts
- Entertainment
- ABC Studios
- Master Key Production

Pres.
No.108

PRESIDENT HENRY ROARKE
"Quantico"
2017
Played by
Dennis Boutsikaris

- briefing staff [p.99]
- broadcast on TV [p.103]
- giving a press conference [p.148]
- giving a speech [p.155]
- in a conversation [p.195]
- on TV [p.302]
- reading files [p.316]

Produced by
- The Mark Gordon Company
- Random Acts
- Entertainment
- ABC Studios
- Master Key Production

Pres.
No.109

PRESIDENT JACK DAVIS
"Revolution"
2014
Played by
Cotter Smith

- as a hostage [p.58]
- giving a speech [p.153]
- injured [p.249]
- shaking hands [p.332]
- waving [p.387]

Produced by
- Kripke Enterprises
- Bad Robot
- Warner Bros. Television

Pres.
No.110

PRESIDENT HOWARD LEWIS
"Salt"
2010
Played by
Hunt Block

- at a funeral [p.63]
- being briefed [p.83]
- broadcast on TV [p.101]
- fighting [p.124]
- fleeing [p.127]
- giving a speech [p.154]
- hiding [p.172]
- in a bunker [p.181]
- in a control center [p.188]
- in a conversation [p.193]
- in a meeting [p.205]
- in an elevator [p.225]
- on the telephone [p.292]
- reading files [p.314]
- threatened with a weapon [p.375]
- under fire [p.379]
- with the nuclear briefcase [p.417]
- with the nuclear code [p.419]
- with the Secret Service [p.424]

Produced by
- Columbia Pictures
- Relativity Media
- Di Bonaventura Pictures
- Wintergreen Productions

Pres.
No.111

PRESIDENT PAULINE MACKENZIE
"Salvation"
2017
Played by
Tovah Feldshuh

- addressing the nation on TV [p.52]
- behind the desk in the Oval Office [p.73]
- behind her desk in the Oval Office, talking to the staff [p.78]
- being briefed [p.83]
- briefing staff [p.97]
- broadcast on TV [p.101]
- frustrated [p.130]
- in a bunker [p.181]
- in a conversation [p.193]
- in a meeting at the Oval Office [p.209]
- in a meeting with the military [p.215]
- in the hospital [p.235]
- on TV [p.300]
- reading files [p.314]
- saluting [p.323]
- shaking hands [p.332]
- sitting on the desk in the Oval Office [p.350]
- with the nuclear briefcase [p.417]
- with the nuclear code [p.419]

Produced by
- Secret Hideout
- Still Married Productions
- CBS Television Studios

Pres.
No.112

PRESIDENT MONROE BENNETT
"Salvation"
2017
Played by
Sasha Roiz

- as a hostage [p.58]
- behind the desk in the Oval Office [p.74]
- behind his desk in the Oval Office, talking to the staff [p.78]
- being sworn in [p.87]
- broadcast on TV [p.101]
- in a conversation [p.193]
- in a meeting [p.206]
- in the Oval Office talking to the staff [p.242]
- on TV [p.300]
- signing files [p.344]
- sitting behind the desk addressing the nation [p.348]
- threatened with a weapon [p.375]
- with the nuclear briefcase [p.418]
- with the nuclear code [p.420]
- with the officer who is carrying the nuclear briefcase [p.422]

Produced by
- Secret Hideout
- Still Married Productions
- CBS Television Studio

Pres.
No.113

PRESIDENT FITZGERALD GRANT
"Scandal"
2012–2017
Played by
Jeff Perry

- addressing Congress [p.50]
- at the inauguration [p.68]
- behind the desk in the Oval Office [p.74]
- being sworn in [p.87]
- dancing [p.107]
- drinking alcohol [p.114]
- getting out of a helicopter [p.139]
- in a conversation [p.193]
- in the hospital [p.235]
- in the Oval Office talking to the staff [p.242]
- injured [p.249]
- kissing his mistress [p.253]
- looking out the window of the Oval Office [p.289]
- on TV [p.300]
- out for a cake [p.302]
- reading files [p.315]
- targeted by a gun [p.371]
- under fire [p.379]
- with his mistress [p.412]
- with his wife [p.414]

Produced by
- Shondaland
- ABC Studios

Pres.
No.114

PRESIDENT SALLY LANGSTON
"Scandal"
2012–2013
Played by
Kate Burton

- behind the desk in the Oval Office [p.74]
- behind her desk in the Oval Office, talking to the staff [p.78]
- being sworn in [p.87]
- briefing staff [p.97]
- broadcast on TV [p.101]
- in a conversation [p.193]
- in a meeting at the Oval Office [p.209]
- in the Oval Office talking to the staff [p.242]

• in the Situation Room [p. 246]
• looking at a screen [p. 261]
• on the telephone [p. 292]
• on TV [p. 300]
• signing files [p. 344]
• working [p. 426]

Produced by
• Shondaland
• ABC Studios

Pres. No. 115

PRESIDENT MELLIE GRANT
"Scandal"
2017–2018
Played by
Bellamy Young

• arguing [p. 55]
• at a banquet [p. 61]
• at a state reception [p. 66]
• at the inauguration [p. 68]
• behind the desk in the Oval Office [p. 74]
• behind her desk in the Oval Office, talking to the staff [p. 78]
• being briefed [p. 84]
• being sworn in [p. 87]
• drinking alcohol [p. 114]
• getting dressed [p. 134]
• giving a speech [p. 154]
• in a conversation [p. 193]
• in a meeting [p. 206]
• in a meeting at the Oval Office [p. 210]
• looking shocked at a screen [p. 271]
• meeting another politician [p. 274]
• on TV [p. 300]
• photographed by the press [p. 305]
• signing files [p. 344]
• targeted by a gun [p. 371]
• waving [p. 387]
• working on a computer [p. 430]

Produced by
• Shondaland
• ABC Studios

Pres. No. 116

PRESIDENT BAXTER HARRIS
"Scary Movie 3"
2003
Played by
Leslie Nielsen

• behind his desk in the Oval Office, talking to the staff [p. 78]
• being briefed [p. 84]
• fighting [p. 124]
• fleeing [p. 127]
• getting into a car [p. 136]
• giving a speech [p. 154]
• helpless [p. 170]
• in a conversation [p. 193]
• listening to music [p. 256]
• looking at a painting [p. 259]
• looking out the window of the Oval Office [p. 269]
• reading files [p. 315]
• scared [p. 326]
• screaming [p. 328]
• waving [p. 387]
• with a bridal bouquet [p. 390]
• with an alien [p. 403]
• with the Secret Service [p. 424]

Produced by
• Dimension Films
• Brad Grey Pictures
• John Thomas Special FX

Pres. No. 117

PRESIDENT BAXTER HARRIS
"Scary Movie 4"
2006
Played by
Leslie Nielsen

• at the United Nations [p. 69]
• being briefed [p. 84]
• briefing staff [p. 97]
• drinking milk [p. 116]
• drinking water [p. 117]
• giving a speech at the United Nations naked [p. 156]
• in a school class [p. 218]
• in bed [p. 228]
• naked [p. 275]

Produced by
• Dimension Films
• 415 Project
• Brad Grey Pictures
• Miramax
• Scary Movie 4

Pres. No. 118

PRESIDENT NELSON
"Scorcher"
2002
Played by
Rutger Hauer

• behind the desk in the Oval Office [p. 74]
• being briefed [p. 84]
• boarding Air Force One [p. 93]
• briefing staff [p. 97]
• broadcast on TV [p. 101]
• looking at military strategies [p. 265]
• looking out the window of the Oval Office [p. 269]
• looking shocked at a screen [p. 271]
• saluting [p. 324]
• sitting behind the desk addressing the nation [p. 348]

Produced by
• Cinetel Films4

Pres. No. 119

PRESIDENT JORDAN LYMAN
"Seven Days in May"
1964
Played by
Fredric March

• behind the desk in the Oval Office [p. 74]
• behind his desk in the Oval Office, talking to the staff [p. 79]
• being briefed [p. 84]
• broadcast on TV [p. 101]
• drinking alcohol [p. 114]
• drinking water [p. 116]
• giving a speech [p. 154]
• in a bathrobe [p. 180]
• in a conversation [p. 1924]
• in a meeting [p. 206]
• in a video conference [p. 222]
• on the telephone [p. 292]
• on TV [p. 300]
• reading files [p. 315]
• reading the newspaper [p. 318]
• smoking [p. 355]
• thoughtful [p. 373]
• with a doctor [p. 395]

Produced by
• Joel Productions
• Seven Arts Productions

Pres. No. 120

PRESIDENT MARCUS ROBBINS
"Sharknado 3 – Oh Hell No!"
2015
Played by
Mark Cuban

• awarding an officer [p. 70]
• giving a speech [p. 154]
• in a bunker [p. 181]
• in an elevator [p. 225]
• injured [p. 249]
• with a gun [p. 400]

Produced by
• Syfy
• The Asylum
• Sonatina
• Ventana Productions
• M ss ng p eces

Pres. No. 121

THE PRESIDENT OF THE UNITED STATES OF AMERICA
"Shooter"
2007
Played by
Tom Butler

• giving a speech [p. 154]
• greeting a crowd [p. 159]
• on TV [p. 300]
• targeted by a gun [p. 371]
• under fire [p. 379]

Produced by
• Paramount Pictures
• Di Bonaventura Pictures
• Grosvenor Park Impact Productions

Pres. No. 122

PRESIDENT LEX LUTHOR
"Smallville"
2001
Played by
Michael Rosenbaum

• on TV [p. 300]

Produced by
• Tollin
• Robbins Productions
• Millar Gough Ink
• Warner Bros. Television
• DC Comics
• DC Entertainment
• Smallville 3 Films
• Smallville Films
• Tollin/Robbins Productions
• Warner Bros.

Pres. No. 123

THE PRESIDENT OF THE UNITED STATES OF AMERICA
"Spy Kids 3-D"
2003
Played by
George Clooney

• in a video conference [p. 222]

Produced by
• Dimension Films
• Los Hooligans Productions
• Troublemaker Studios

Pres. No. 124

PRESIDENT HENRY HAYES
"Stargate SG-1"
2004
Played by
William Devaney

• behind the desk in the Oval Office [p. 74]
• behind his desk in the Oval Office, talking to the staff [p. 79]
• being briefed [p. 84]
• in a conversation [p. 194]
• in a meeting at the Oval Office [p. 210]
• in a meeting with the military [p. 215]
• in the Oval Office talking to the staff [p. 242]
• looking in the mirror [p. 266]
• reading files [p. 315]
• taking his shoes off [p. 358]
• watching TV [p. 384]

- with a Lincoln bust [p.391]
- working late [p.429]

Produced by
- Double Secret Productions
- Gekko Film Corp.
- Kawoosh! Productions IX
- Kawoosh! Productions VII
- MGM Worldwide Television Productions
- Sony Pictures Television
- Stargate SG-1 Production (II) Inc.

Pres.
No.125

PRESIDENT
CONSTANCE PAYTON
"State of Affairs"
2014–2015
Played by
Alfre Woodard

- at a funeral [p.63]
- at a graveyard [p.64]
- behind the desk in the Oval Office [p.74]
- behind her desk in the Oval Office, talking to the staff [p.79]
- drinking alcohol [p.114]
- giving a press conference [p.148]
- giving a speech [p.154]
- having dinner [p.168]
- in a car [p.185]
- in a conversation [p.194]
- in a meeting at the Oval Office [p.210]
- in the Oval Office talking to the staff [p.243]
- on TV [p.300]
- reading files [p.315]
- shooting [p.338]
- sitting on the desk in the Oval Office [p.350]
- with a gun [p.400]

Produced by
- Aardwolf Creative
- STX Entertainment
- Abishag Productions
- Universal Television

Pres.
No.126

PRESIDENT WESTWOOD
"Stealth Fighter"
1999
Played by
Ernie Hudson

- being briefed [p.84]
- briefing staff [p.97]
- in a car [p.186]
- in a conversation [p.194]
- in a meeting [p.206]
- looking at military strategies [p.265]
- on the telephone [p.292]
- reading files [p.315]

Produced by
- Cinetel Films
- Artisan Entertainment
- Grey Matter Entertainment
- Stealth Fighter Pictures

Pres.
No.127

THE PRESIDENT OF THE UNITED STATES OF AMERICA
"Suddenly"
2013
Played by
Chris Shields

- getting out of the car [p.144]
- giving a speech [p.154]
- on TV [p.300]
- under fire [p.379]

Produced by
- Canadian Film or Video Production Tax Credit
- Nasser Entertainment Group
- Odyssey Media
- Province of British Columbia Film Incentive BC

Pres.
No.128

PRESIDENT
OLIVIA MARSDIN
"Supergirl"
2015–2017
Played by
Lynda Carter

- as an alien [p.59]
- fleeing [p.127]
- getting into a car [p.136]
- getting out of Air Force One [p.140]
- getting out of Air Force One, waving [p.142]
- giving a speech [p.154]
- greeting a crowd [p.159]
- in a conversation [p.194]
- in a meeting [p.206]
- in a video conference [p.222]
- in the office on board Air Force One [p.240]
- on board Air Force One [p.283]
- under fire [p.379]
- with a superhero [p.405]

Produced by
- Berlanti Productions
- Warner Bros. Television

Pres.
No.129

PRESIDENT
ANDREW BOONE
"Swing Vote"
2008
Played by
Kelsey Grammer

- angry [p.54]
- behind the desk in the Oval Office [p.74]
- briefing staff [p.98]
- drinking alcohol [p.114]
- gambling [p.131]
- getting out of Air Force One [p.141]
- giving a speech [p.154]
- in a conversation [p.194]
- in a meeting [p.206]
- in a meeting at the Oval Office [p.210]
- in the office on board Air Force One [p.240]
- looking in the mirror [p.267]
- on a stage [p.280]
- on board Air Force One [p.283]
- on the telephone [p.292]
- shaking hands [p.332]
- watching TV [p.384]
- working [p.426]

Produced by
- Touchstone Pictures
- Radar Pictures
- 1821 Pictures
- Treehouse Films (II)
- Tig Productions
- G&M Films

Pres.
No.130

PRESIDENT WIDMARK
"The Adventures of Buckaroo Banzai Across the 8th Dimension"
1984
Played by
Ronald Lacey

- being briefed [p.84]
- broadcast on TV [p.101]
- in a crisis situation [p.197]
- in bed [p.228]
- looking in the mirror [p.267]
- on TV [p.300]
- reading a note [p.311]
- reading files [p.315]
- watching TV [p.384]

Produced by
- Sherwood Productions

Pres.
No.131

PRESIDENT FALLBROOK
"The Alternate"
2000
Played by
John Beck

- as a hostage [p.58]
- being briefed [p.84]
- drinking coffee [p.112]
- fighting [p.124]
- fleeing [p.127]
- getting out of the car [p.144]
- giving a speech [p.154]
- hugging his wife [p.176]
- in a car [p.186]
- in a conversation [p.194]
- in a restaurant kitchen [p.217]
- in an elevator [p.225]
- kissing [p.252]
- on the cell phone [p.287]
- on TV [p.300]
- talking to the press [p.369]
- threatened with a weapon [p.375]
- waving [p.387]
- with his wife [p.414]

Produced by
- Millennium Films

Pres.
No.132

PRESIDENT
ANDREW SHEPHERD
"The American President"
1995
Played by
Michael Douglas

- at a banquet [p.61]
- at a state reception [p.66]
- behind his desk in the Oval Office, talking to the staff [p.79]
- being briefed [p.84]
- dancing [p.107]
- drinking coffee [p.112]
- drinking alcohol [p.114]
- getting dressed [p.134]
- giving a press conference [p.149]
- greeting a crowd [p.159]
- greeting guests at a banquet [p.162]
- having dinner [p.168]
- in a car [p.185]
- in a conversation [p.194]
- in a meeting [p.206]
- in a meeting at the Oval Office [p.210]
- in bed [p.228]
- in the Oval Office talking to the staff [p.243]
- kissing [p.252]
- on the telephone [p.292]
- on TV [p.300]
- playing pool [p.309]
- reading a note [p.311]
- reading files [p.315]
- screaming [p.328]
- shaking hands [p.332]
- walking outside the Oval Office [p.381]
- working [p.426]

Produced by
- Universal Pictures
- Castle Rock Entertainment
- Wildwood Enterprises
- Columbia Pictures
- Digital Image Associates

Pres.
No.133

PRESIDENT
ART HOCKSTADER
“The Best Man”
1964
Played by Lee Tracy

• drinking alcohol [p.115]
• in a conversation [p.194]
• laughing [p.254]
• reading files [p.315]

Produced by
• Millar/Turman Productions

Pres.
No.134

PRESIDENT
LAWRENCE RANDOLPH
“The Brady Bunch in the White House”
2002
Played by
Dave Nichols

• being sworn in [p.87]
• giving a press conference [p.149]
• shocked [p.337]

Produced by
• Paramount Network Television Productions
• Paramount Television
• Redwood Productions

Pres.
No.135

PRESIDENT
MIKE BRADY
“The Brady Bunch in the White House”
2002
Played by Gary Cole

• addressing Congress [p.50]
• at a banquet [p.61]
• at the inauguration [p.68]
• behind the desk in the Oval Office [p.74]
• behind his desk in the Oval Office, talking to the staff [p.79]
• being briefed [p.84]
• being sworn in [p.87]
• broadcast on TV [p.101]
• dancing [p.107]
• giving a press conference [p.149]
• giving a speech [p.154]
• hanging a picture in the Oval Office [p.164]
• in a bathrobe [p.180]
• in a meeting [p.206]
• in a meeting at the Oval Office [p.210]
• in an elevator [p.226]
• in bed with his wife [p.232]
• in the newspaper [p.238]
• in the Oval Office talking to the staff [p.243]
• kissing [p.252]
• looking out the window of the Oval Office [p.269]
• reading files [p.315]
• signing files [p.344]
• sitting behind the desk addressing the nation [p.348]
• with his wife [p.414]

Produced by
• Paramount Network Television Productions
• Paramount Television
• Redwood Productions

Pres.
No.136

PRESIDENT
JULIAN NAVARRO
“The Brink”
2015
Played by
Esai Morales

• drinking coffee [p.112]
• in a conversation [p.194]
• in a meeting [p.206]
• in a video conference [p.222]
• on the telephone [p.292]
• reading files [p.315]

Produced by
• Everyman Pictures
• Home Box Office
• Jerry Weintraub Productions

Pres.
No.137

PRESIDENT
JACKSON EVANS
“The Contender”
2000
Played by
Jeff Bridges

• addressing Congress [p.50]
• behind the desk in the Oval Office [p.74]
• behind his desk in the Oval Office, talking to the staff [p.79]
• bowling [p.95]
• eating a sandwich [p.119]
• giving a speech [p.154]
• greeting a crowd [p.159]
• greeting guests at a banquet [p.162]
• in a meeting at the Oval Office [p.210]
• in a tracksuit [p.219]
• making smoke rings [p.272]
• meeting another politician [p.274]
• out for a hike [p.303]
• shaking hands [p.333]
• sitting on the desk in the Oval Office [p.350]
• smoking [p.355]
• with feet on the table [p.407]

Produced by
• Cinerenta Medien-beteiligungs KG
• Cinecontender
• Battleground Productions
• SE8 Group
• Battlefield

Pres.
No.138

PRESIDENT BLAKE
“The Day After Tomorrow”
2004
Played by
Perry King

• behind the desk in the Oval Office [p.74]
• in a meeting [p.207]
• on the telephone [p.292]
• watching TV [p.384]

Produced by
• Twentieth Century Fox
• Centropolis Entertainment
• Lions Gate Films
• Mark Gordon Productions
• Mel’s Cite du Cinema

Pres.
No.139

PRESIDENT BECKER
“The Day After Tomorrow”
2004
Played by
Kenneth Welsh

• addressing the nation on TV [p.53]
• on TV [p.301]

Produced by
• Twentieth Century Fox
• Centropolis Entertainment
• Lions Gate Films
• Mark Gordon Productions
• Mel’s Cite du Cinema

Pres.
No.140

PRESIDENT LINDBERG
“The Fifth Element”
1997
Played by
Thomas Lister Jr.

• being briefed [p.84]
• briefing staff [p.98]
• drinking alcohol [p.115]
• in a conversation [p.194]
• in the Situation Room [p.226]
• on the cell phone [p.287]
• on the telephone [p.292]
• reading files [p.315]
• scared [p.326]
• smiling [p.353]

Produced by
• Gaumont

Pres.
No.141

PRESIDENT
WILLIAM JOHNSON
“The First Family”
2012–2015
Played by
Christopher B. Duncan

• behind the desk in the Oval Office [p.74]
• behind his desk in the Oval Office, talking to the staff [p.79]
• kissing [p.252]
• wearing sunglasses [p.389]
• with his daughter [p.409]
• with his family [p.412]
• with his wife [p.414]

Produced by
• Entertainment Studios

Pres.
No.142

PRESIDENT
ADAM SCOTT
“The Kidnapping of the President”
1980
Played by
Hal Holbrook

• as a hostage [p.58]
• behind the desk in the Oval Office [p.74]
• behind his desk in the Oval Office, talking to the staff [p.79]
• getting out of Air Force One [p.141]
• getting out of Air Force One, waving [p.142]
• getting out of the car [p.145]
• greeting a crowd [p.159]
• in a car [p.186]
• in a conversation [p.194]
• in a meeting at the Oval Office [p.210]
• in the office on board Air Force One [p.240]
• in the Oval Office talking to the staff [p.243]
• looking out the window of the Oval Office [p.269]
• on board Air Force One [p.283]
• on the telephone [p.292]
• reading files [p.315]
• signing files [p.344]
• talking to his wife [p.365]
• threatened with a weapon [p.375]

Produced by
• Presidential Films
• Sefel Films

Pres.
No.143

PRESIDENT
KELLY GELLER
"The Last Ship"
2014
Played by
Deborah May

• addressing the nation on TV [p.53]

Produced by
• Channel Road Productions
• Platinum Dunes
• TNT Originals

Pres.
No.144

PRESIDENT
JEFFREY MICHENER
"The Last Ship"
2015–2016
Played by
Mark Moses

• behind the desk in the Oval Office [p.75]
• behind his desk in the Oval Office, talking to the staff [p.79]
• being briefed [p.84]
• briefing staff [p.98]
• broadcast on TV [p.101]
• eating [p.120]
• in a control center [p.188]
• in a conversation [p.194]
• in a meeting with the military [p.215]
• looking shocked at a screen [p.258]
• looking at military strategies [p.265]
• looking at a screen [p.271]
• on board a ship [p.284]
• reading files [p.315]

Produced by
• Channel Road Productions
• Platinum Dunes
• TNT Originals

Pres.
No.145

PRESIDENT
THOMAS WESTWOOD
"The Lottery"
2014
Played by
Yul Vazquez

• addressing the nation on TV [p.53]
• broadcast on TV [p.101]
• giving a speech [p.154]
• in a meeting [p.207]
• in a meeting room [p.213]
• looking out the window of the Oval Office [p.269]
• on TV [p.301]

Produced by
• Grady Twins Productions
• Warner Horizon Television

Pres.
No.146

PRESIDENT
DOUGLASS DILMAN
"The Man"
1972
Played by
James Earl Jones

• behind the desk in the Oval Office [p.75]
• being briefed [p.84]
• giving a press conference [p.149]
• giving a speech [p.155]
• in a meeting [p.207]
• in a meeting at the Oval Office [p.210]

Produced by
• ABC Circle Films
• Lorimar Productions

Pres.
No.147

PRESIDENT
JOHN BALLENTINE
"The Sentinel"
2006
Played by
David Rasche

• at a state reception [p.66]
• behind his desk in the Oval Office, talking to the staff [p.79]
• being briefed [p.85]
• boarding a helicopter [p.91]
• fleeing [p.127]
• getting out of the car [p.145]
• giving a press conference [p.149]
• giving a speech [p.155]
• greeting a crowd [p.159]
• in a car [p.186]
• in a conversation [p.194]
• in a helicopter [p.200]
• in a meeting at the Oval Office [p.210]
• in a restaurant kitchen [p.217]
• meeting another politician [p.274]
• on TV [p.301]
• out for a hike [p.303]
• reading files [p.316]
• shaking hands [p.333]
• signing files [p.344]
• talking to his wife [p.365]
• walking outside the Oval Office [p.381]
• waving [p.388]

Produced by
• Twentieth Century Fox
• Regency Enterprises
• Epsilon Motion Pictures
• Furthur Films
• New Regency Pictures
• Dune Entertainment
• Major Studio Partners
• Sentinel Productions

Pres.
No.148

PRESIDENT
J. ROBERT FOWLER
"The Sum of All Fears"
2002
Played by
James Cromwell

• bloodied [p.89]
• briefing staff [p.98]
• fleeing [p.127]
• getting into a car [p.137]
• giving a speech [p.155]
• helpless [p.170]
• in a bunker [p.182]
• in a car [p.186]
• in a control center [p.189]
• in a crisis situation [p.197]
• in a meeting [p.207]
• injured [p.249]
• on board Air Force One [p.283]
• on the telephone [p.293]
• on TV [p.301]
• out for a hike [p.3031]
• saluting [p.324]
• screaming [p.328]
• shaking hands [p.333]
• signing files [p.444]
• thoughtful [p.373]
• waving [p.388]
• with the nuclear code [p.420]
• with the officer who is carrying the nuclear briefcase [p.422]

Produced by
• Paramount Pictures
• Mace Neufeld Productions
• MFP Munich Film Partners GmbH & Company I. Produktions KG
• Mel's Cite du Cinema
• S.O.A.F. Productions

Pres.
No.149

PRESIDENT
P.J. AIMES
"The Summit"
2008
Played by
Christopher Plummer

• being briefed [p.85]
• briefing staff [p.98]
• drinking alcohol [p.115]
• drinking water [p.118]
• greeting foreign politicians [p.160]
• in a conversation [p.195]
• in the hospital [p.235]
• in the Situation Room [p.246]
• looking at a screen [p.261]
• meeting another politician [p.274]
• photographed by the press [p.305]
• playing golf [p.308]
• screaming [p.329]
• smiling [p.355]
• talking to the press [p.369]

Produced by
• FH & S Productions
• Media Headquarters
• Shaftesbury Films

Pres.
No.150

PRESIDENT
JOSIAH BARTLET
"The West Wing"
1999–2006
Played by
Martin Sheen

• behind the desk in the Oval Office [p.75]
• behind his desk in the Oval Office, talking to the staff [p.79]
• being briefed [p.85]
• drinking coffee [p.112]
• drinking alcohol [p.115]
• giving a speech [p.155]
• in a conversation [p.195]
• in a meeting [p.207]
• in a meeting at the Oval Office [p.210]
• in the Oval Office talking to the staff [p.243]
• playing basketball [p.307]
• reading a note [p.311]
• reading files [p.316]
• shaking hands [p.333]
• with a doctor [p.399]

Produced by
• John Wells Productions
• Warner Bros. Television

Pres.
No.151

PRESIDENT
DAVID STEVENS
"Twilight's Last Gleaming"
1977
Played by
Charles Durning

• as a hostage [p.58]
• behind his desk in the Oval Office, talking to the staff [p.79]
• dead [p.209]
• drinking alcohol [p.115]
• getting out of Air Force One [p.141]
• greeting the military [p.163]
• in a bunker [p.182]
• in a car [p.186]
• in a conversation [p.195]
• in a meeting at the Oval Office [p.210]
• looking out the window of the Oval Office [p.269]
• on the telephone [p.293]
• reading files [p.316]

• shaking hands [p. 333]
• shaving [p. 335]
• shocked [p. 337]
• shot [p. 340]
• targeted by a gun [p. 371]
• threatened with a weapon [p. 376]

Produced by
• Bavaria Atelier
• Bavaria Film
• Geria Productions
• Lorimar Productions

Pres. No. 152

PRESIDENT MAXWELL MONROE
"Under Siege"
1992
Played by Hal Holbrook

• giving a speech [p. 155]

Produced by
• Warner Bros.
• Regency Enterprises
• Canal+
• Alcor Films
• Arnon Milchan Productions

Pres. No. 153

PRESIDENT HARRY ASHTON
"Vantage Point"
2008
Played by William Hurt

• as a hostage [p. 58]
• being briefed [p. 85]
• bloodied [p. 89]
• broadcast on TV [p. 101]
• getting into a car [p. 137]
• getting out of the car [p. 145]
• giving a speech [p. 155]
• greeting a crowd [p. 159]
• in a car [p. 186]
• injured [p. 249]
• meeting another politician [p. 274]
• on a stage [p. 280]
• on the cell phone [p. 287]
• on the telephone [p. 293]
• on TV [p. 301]
• photographed by the press [p. 305]
• reading files [p. 316]
• shot [p. 341]
• targeted by a gun [p. 371]
• threatened with a weapon [p. 376]
• watching TV [p. 385]

Produced by
• Production Companies
• Columbia Pictures
• Relativity Media
• Original Film
• Art In Motion
• Kanzaman

Pres. No. 154

PRESIDENT SELINA MEYER
"Veep"
2016–2017
Played by Julia Louis-Dreyfus

• addressing Congress [p. 50]
• behind her desk in the Oval Office, talking to the staff [p. 79]
• being briefed [p. 85]
• briefing staff [p. 98]
• greeting a crowd [p. 159]
• in a meeting at the Oval Office [p. 210]
• in a meeting with the military [p. 215]
• on a phone screen [p. 276]

Produced by
• HBO Entertainment
• Dundee Productions

Pres. No. 155

PRESIDENT LAURA P. MONTEZ
"Veep"
2017
Played by Andrea Savage

• behind her desk in the Oval Office, talking to the staff [p. 79]
• briefing staff [p. 93]
• giving a speech [p. 155]
• in a meeting at the Oval Office [p. 210]
• on TV [p. 301]

Produced by
• HBO Entertainment
• Dundee Productions

Pres. No. 156

PRESIDENT RICHARDSON
"Virus"
1980
Played by Glenn Ford

• behind his desk in the Oval Office, talking to the staff [p. 75]
• behind the desk in the Oval Office [p. 80]
• briefing staff [p. 98]
• in a meeting at the Oval Office [p. 211]
• looking at military strategies [p. 265]
• on the red telephone [p. 288]
• on the telephone [p. 293]
• watching TV [p. 385]

Produced by
• Haruki Kadokawa Office

Pres. No. 157

PRESIDENT MONROE COLE
"Welcome to Mooseport"
2004
Played by Gene Hackman

• being briefed [p. 85]
• drinking alcohol [p. 115]
• getting out of the car [p. 145]
• giving a speech [p. 155]
• having breakfast [p. 166]
• in a car [p. 186]
• in a conversation [p. 195]
• in a tracksuit [p. 219]
• on board Air Force One [p. 283]
• on the telephone [p. 293]
• on TV [p. 301]
• playing golf [p. 308]
• reading files [p. 316]
• reading the newspaper [p. 318]
• shaking hands [p. 333]
• watching TV [p. 385]
• waving [p. 388]
• with a dog [p. 398]
• working out [p. 432]

Produced by
• Twentieth Century Fox
• Intermedia Films
• Mediastream Vierte Film GmbH & Co. Vermarktungs KG
• Mooseport Productions

Pres. No. 158

PRESIDENT JAMES W. SAWYER
"White House Down"
2013
Played by Jamie Foxx

• as a hostage [p. 58]
• behind his desk in the Oval Office, talking to the staff [p. 80]
• boarding a helicopter [p. 91]
• fleeing [p. 127]
• getting into a car [p. 137]
• getting out of a helicopter [p. 139]
• in a bunker [p. 182]
• in a car [p. 186]
• in a conversation [p. 195]
• in a helicopter [p. 200]
• injured [p. 249]
• on a phone screen [p. 276]
• on the cell phone [p. 287]
• on TV [p. 301]
• saluting [p. 324]
• shaking hands [p. 333]
• shooting [p. 339]
• shot [p. 341]
• threatened with a weapon [p. 376]
• under fire [p. 379]
• with a gun [p. 400]

Produced by
• Columbia Pictures
• Mythology Entertainment
• Centropolis Entertainment
• Iron Horse Entertainment (II)

Pres. No. 159

PRESIDENT ALVIN HAMMOND
"White House Down"
2013
Played by Michael Murphy

• being sworn in [p. 87]

Produced by
• Columbia Pictures
• Mythology Entertainment
• Centropolis Entertainment
• Iron Horse Entertainment (II)

Pres. No. 160

PRESIDENT BARBARA ADAMS
"Whoops Apocalypse"
1986
Played by Loretta Swit

• at a state reception [p. 66]
• behind her desk in the Oval Office, talking to the staff [p. 80]
• broadcast on TV [p. 101]
• drinking water [p. 118]
• getting out of a helicopter [p. 139]
• giving a press conference [p. 149]
• giving a speech [p. 155]
• in a bathrobe [p. 180]
• in a car [p. 186]
• in a meeting at the Oval Office [p. 211]
• in bed [p. 228]
• on the telephone [p. 293]
• reading files [p. 316]
• swimming [p. 357]
• talking to an inmate [p. 361]

Produced by
• Incorporated Television Company
• Picture Partnership

Pres. No. 161

PRESIDENT LOCKWOOD
"Wrong is Right"
1982
Played by George Grizzard

• behind the desk in the Oval Office [p. 75]
• being briefed [p. 85]
• briefing staff [p. 98]
• broadcast on TV [p. 101]
• getting out of the car [p. 145]
• giving a speech [p. 155]

• in a control center [p.189]
• in a conversation [p.195]
• in a helicopter [p.200]
• in a meeting [p.207]
• in a tracksuit [p.220]
• looking at a screen [p.261]
• looking at military strategies [p.265]
• on the telephone [p.293]
• on TV [p.301]
• reading files [p.316]
• screaming [p.329]
• sitting behind the desk addressing the nation [p.348]
• watching TV [p.385]
• with a dog [p.398]
• with the nuclear briefcase [p.418]
• with the officer who is carrying the nuclear briefcase [p.422]
• with the Secret Service [p.424]
• working out [p.432]

Produced by
• Columbia Pictures
• Rastar Productions

Pres.
No.162

PRESIDENT
GEORGE MCKENNA
"X-Men 2"
2003
Played by
Cotter Smith

• behind the desk in the Oval Office [p.75]
• broadcast on TV [p.102]
• drinking alcohol [p.115]
• fighting [p.124]
• fleeing [p.127]
• hiding [p.172]
• in a meeting at the Oval Office [p.211]
• looking out the window of the Oval Office [p.269]
• reading files [p.316]

Produced by
• Twentieth Century Fox
• Marvel Enterprises
• Donners' Company
• Bad Hat Harry Productions
• XF2 Canada Productions
• XM2 Productions

Pres.
No.163

MR. PRESIDENT
"X-Men 3: The Last Stand"
2006
Played by
Josef Sommer

• behind the desk in the Oval Office [p.75]
• behind his desk in the Oval Office, talking to the staff [p.80]
• being briefed [p.85]
• in a conversation [p.195]
• in a meeting [p.207]
• in a video conference [p.222]
• looking shocked at a screen [p.271]
• on TV [p.301]
• reading files [p.316]
• screaming [p.329]
• watching TV [p.385]
• with an alien [p.403]

Produced by
• Twentieth Century Fox
• Marvel Enterprises
• Donners' Company
• Ingenious Film Partners
• Dune Entertainment
• Major Studio Partners
• Bad Hat Harry Productions
• X3 Canada Productions
• X3US Productions
• XM3 Service thinkfilm

Pres.
No.164

PRESIDENT
JAMES STANFORD
"XXX: State of the Union"
2005
Played by
Peter Strauss

• addressing Congress [p.50]
• as a hostage [p.58]
• awarding an officer [p.70]
• being briefed [p.85]
• fighting [p.124]
• getting out of the car [p.145]
• greeting a crowd [p.159]
• in a conversation [p.195]
• in a meeting at the Oval Office [p.211]
• in the Oval Office talking to the staff [p.243]
• on TV [p.301]
• reading files [p.316]
• targeted by a gun [p.376]
• waving [p.388]

Produced by
• Columbia Pictures
• Revolution Studios
• Original Film

Imprint

Concept and design:
Lea N. Michel

Published by Scheidegger & Spiess in cooperation with the Institut für Buchkunst Leipzig, Prof. Ludovic Balland, Julia Blume

Essay: Teresa Rudolf

Translation:
Mark Willard, Tradukas

Proofreading:
Colette Forder

Image editing:
Widmer & Fluri

Printing and binding:
DZA Druckerei zu Altenburg GmbH, Thuringia

Fonts:
IBM Plex Mono, Starling

Paper:
Multi Offset 110 g/m², 350 g/m²

Verlag
Scheidegger & Spiess
Niederdorfstrasse 54
8001 Zurich
Switzerland
www.scheidegger-spiess.ch

Scheidegger & Spiess is being supported by the Federal Office of Culture with a general subsidy for the years 2016–2020.

ISBN 978-3-85881-858-4

Diploma project by
Lea N. Michel
submitted at the Academy of Fine Arts, Leipzig

Supervised by:
Prof. Maureen Mooren
Prof. Ludovic Balland
Birtt Helbig

Special thanks to:
Mona-Lisa Michel
Alex Michel
Franziska Müller
Margit Schaal
Heidy Michel
Hans Michel
Daytona Häusermann
Nicole Imhof
Lhamo Meyer
Janna Gribi
Milena Meier
Louisa Gagliardi
Benjamin Buchegger
Christian Hofer
Katharina Schilling
Benjamin Ganz
Tim Wetter
Immo Schneider
Jasper Eisenecker
Jan Sattler
Lukas Schimpfhauser
Teresa Rudolf
Teresa Schönherr
Hanna Stiegeler
Maureen Mooren
Britt Helbig
Ludovic Balland
Julia Blume
Johannes Oestringer
Andre Grau
Lisa Schons
Thomas Kramer
Colette Forder
Lina Morawetz
Tami Komai
Tristam Barrett
Jutamas Rindlisbacher
Ida Michel
Anna Maria Krężel
Dr. Uta Hradetzky
Marianne Wex